ANTONIO'S REVENGE

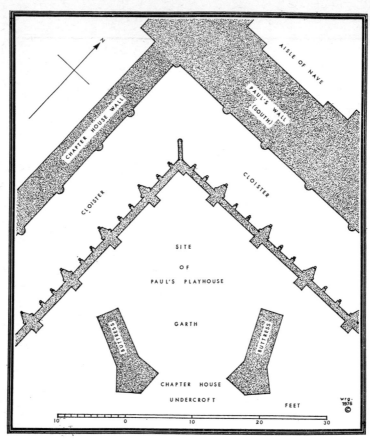

Paul's Boys' Playhouse

THE REVELS PLAYS

ANTONIO'S REVENGE

JOHN MARSTON

Edited by

W. Reavley Gair

MANCHESTER
UNIVERSITY PRESS

THE JOHNS HOPKINS
UNIVERSITY PRESS

Introduction, apparatus criticus, etc.
© W. Reavley Gair, 1978

Manchester University Press
Oxford Road, Manchester M13 9PL
ISBN 0 7190 1501 4

Published in the United States of America, 1978, by
The Johns Hopkins University Press
Baltimore, Maryland 21218
ISBN 0–8018–2012–X

Library of Congress Catalog Card Number 77-4605

British Library Cataloguing in Publication Data

Marston, John
Antonio's revenge.—(The Revels plays).
I. Title II. Gair, W Reavley III. Series
822'.3   PR2694.A5

UK ISBN 0-7190-1501-4
US ISBN 0-8018-2012-X

Printed in Great Britain
by W & J Mackay Limited, Chatham

Contents

General Editor's Preface

The series known as the Revels Plays was conceived by Professor Clifford Leech. The idea emerged in his mind, as he tells us in the General Editor's Preface to the first of the Revels Plays, published in 1958, from the success of the New Arden Shakespeare. The aim of the series was, in his words, 'to apply to Shakespeare's predecessors, contemporaries, and successors the methods that are now used in Shakespeare editing'. We owe it to Clifford Leech that the idea has become reality. He planned the series, set the high standards for it, and for many years selected and supervised the editors. He aimed at editions of lasting merit and usefulness, that would appeal to scholars and students, but not to them alone; producers and actors were also much in his mind. 'The plays included should be such as to deserve and indeed demand performance.' And thus the texts should be presented in a form that is attractive and clear to the actor, with some space of the introduction devoted to records of productions, and some of the notes to comments on stage business.

The text of each Revels Play is edited afresh from the original text (in a few instances, texts) of best authority, but spelling and punctuation are modernised, and speech-headings silently normalised. The text is accompanied by collations and commentary, and in each volume the editor devotes one section of his introduction to a discussion of the provenance and trustworthiness of the 'copytext', the original on which he has based his edition, and to a brief description of particular aspects of his editorial method. Other sections of the introduction deal with the play's date and sources, its place in the work of the author, its significance as a dramatic work of literature in the context of its time and designed for a certain theatre, actors, and audience, its reputation, and its stage-history. In editions of a play by an author not previously represented in the series, it has been customary also to include a brief account of the author's life and career. Some emphasis is laid on providing available records of performances, early and modern.

vii

Modernisation has its problems, and has to be practised with care and some flexibility if the substance of the original is not to be distorted. The editor emends, as distinct from modernising, the original text only in instances where error is patent or at least very probable, and correction persuasive. Archaic forms need sometimes to be retained when rhyme or metre demands them or when a modernised form would alter the required sense or obscure a play on words. The extent to which an editor feels free to adapt the punctuation will largely depend on the degree of authority he attributes to the punctuation of his copy. It is his task to follow the original closely in any dramatic or rhetorical pointing that can be trusted for good reason. Punctuation should do justice to a character's way of speaking, and to the interplay of dialogue.

In general, the manner of modernisation is similar to that in the Arden Shakespeare. Yet in the volumes since 1968, the '-ed' form is used for non-syllabic terminations in past tenses and past participles ('-'d' in Arden and earlier Revels volumes), and '-èd' for syllabic ('-ed' earlier). Act divisions are given only if they appear in the original text or if the structure of the play clearly points to them. Those act and scene divisions not found in the original are provided unobtrusively in small type and in square brackets. Square brackets are also used for any other additions to or changes in the stage directions of the original. But in no instances are directions referring to locale added to scene headings; for the plays (at least those before the Restoration) were designed for stages whose acting area was most of the time neutral and where each scene flowed into the next without interruption; and producers in our time would probably be well advised to attempt to convey this characteristic fluidity of scene on whatever stage they may have at their disposal.

A mixture of principles and common sense also governs the collations accompanying the text. Revels plays do not provide a variorum collation; only those variants which require the critical attention of serious textual students. All departures of substance from 'copy-text' are listed, including any relineation and those changes in punctuation which involve to any degree a decision between alternative interpretations; but not such accidentals as turned letters, nor necessarily additions to stage directions whose editorial nature is already made clear by the use of brackets. Press corrections in the 'copy-texts' are likewise included. Of later emendations of the text (or errors) found in seventeenth-century reprints of no authority or editions from the eighteenth century to modern times, in general only those are given which as alternative readings still deserve serious attention. Readings of a later text of special historical interest of influence are, in some instances, more fully collated.

One of the hallmarks of the Revels Plays is the thoroughness of their annotations. Besides explicating the meaning of difficult words and passages and alerting the reader to special implications, the editor provides comments on customs or usage, text or stage business—indeed on anything he judges pertinent and helpful. Glosses are not provided for words that are satisfactorily explained in simple dictionaries like the *Concise Oxford*. Each volume contains an Index to the Annotations, in which particular attention is drawn to meanings for words not listed in *O.E.D.*

The series began with some of the best-known plays of the Elizabethan and Jacobean era, but has expanded to include also some early Tudor and some Restoration plays. It is moreover not our object to concentrate solely on well-known plays but also to make available some of the lesser known of whose merit as literature and as drama we are convinced.

Early 1976 saw a change in the publisher of the Revels Plays, from Methuen & Co. Ltd to Manchester University Press. By then twenty-three volumes had appeared under the imprint of Methuen. The care with which this distinguished scholarly publishing firm ensured a high quality of book production in the series is only one of many debts some of the editors owe to their long association with Methuen. The news that after a period of uncertainty Manchester University Press has assumed responsibility for the continuation of the series will be welcomed by all students of English drama. Further, I am happy to announce that from now on Professors Ernst Honigmann of the University of Newcastle and J. R. Mulryne of the University of Warwick will join me as general editors of the Revels Plays. These new arrangements should ensure that several volumes planned long ago will soon be published, and that the future direction of the series will be in able hands.

F. DAVID HOENIGER

Toronto, 1977

Note. In this edition Appendix B takes the place of the usual index to the annotations.

Preface

In my General Editors I have been fortunate; initially motivated and encouraged by Professor Clifford Leech, this edition owes a substantial debt to the detailed and informed perusal of Professor David Hoeniger. To the latter is due the credit for a number of illuminating glosses and I am much indebted to his help in the resolution of several thorny problems of interpretation. I owe much to the sympathetic encouragement and scholarship of Professor Muriel Bradbrook; my thanks are due to Professor Harold Jenkins who offered valuable advice on awkward matters of date and sources.

I would like to express my thanks to my colleagues at the University of New Brunswick for many valuable suggestions towards modifying verbal and other obscurities. To libraries and their staffs I am indebted on two continents, but particularly to the inter-library loan department of the University of New Brunswick.

Dr Alistair MacDonald of Acadia University was kind enough to send me a section from his thesis on Marston's stoicism; my typists, Mrs Peggy Pitt and Mrs Diane Goldsmith, have been hard worked and uncomplaining; my wife's enthusiastic encouragement has never flagged.

W.R.G.

Abbreviations

Bullen	*The Works of John Marston*, ed. A. H. Bullen (London, 1887), 2 or 3 vols.
Chambers, *E.S.*	Sir E. K. Chambers, *The Elizabethan Stage* (Oxford, 1923), 4 vols.
E.E.T.S.	*Early English Text Society.*
E.S.	*English Studies.*
Halliwell	*The Works of John Marston*, ed. J. O. Halliwell (London, 1856), 3 vols.
H.L.Q.	*Huntington Library Quarterly.*
Hunter	*Antonio's Revenge*, ed. G. K. Hunter (Lincoln, Nebr., Regents Renaissance Drama, 1965).
Keltie	*The Works of the British Dramatists*, ed. J. S. Keltie (Edinburgh, 1872).
King	A. H. King, *The Language of Satirized Characters in Poetaster* (Lund, *Studies in English*, x, 1941).
Libr.	*The Library.*
M.L.R.	*Modern Language Review.*
M.S.R.	*Malone Society Reprints.*
N. & Q.	*Notes and Queries.*
O.E.D.	*Oxford English Dictionary.*
P.M.L.A.	*Publications of the Modern Language Association of America.*
Q	Quarto.
R.E.S.	*Review of English Studies.*
1633	*The Works of John Marston* (London, 1633).
Sh.Q.	*Shakespeare Quarterly.*
Tilley	M. P. Tilley, *A Dictionary of the Proverbs in England in the Sixteenth and Seventeenth Centuries* (1950).
Wood	*The Plays of John Marston*, ed. H. H. Wood (Edinburgh, 1934–39), 3 vols.

Marston's works are referred to as follows:

I Ant. & Mel.	*The History of Antonio and Mellida, The First Part.*
Ant. Rev.	*Antonio's Revenge.*
Dutch C.	*The Dutch Courtesan.*
Fawn	*Parasitaster, or, The Fawn.*
Histriom.	*Histriomastix.*
Insatiate C.	*The Insatiate Countesse.*
J. Drum's Ent.	*Jack Drum's Entertainment.*
Soph.	*The Wonder of Women or The Tragedie of Sophonisba.*
S.V.	*The Scourge of Villainy.*

Quotations from *I Ant. & Mel., Dutch C., Fawn* and *Malcontent* are taken from the editions in the Regents Renaissance Drama series; all other quotations from Marston's plays are taken from Wood. All quotations from his poems are from the edition by A. Davenport (Liverpool, 1961).

All quotations from Shakespeare are from the *Alexander Shakespeare* (London, 1951) unless otherwise indicated; the line numbering also refers to this edition, and the plays are referred to by Onion's abbreviations (*A Shakespeare Glossary*, 2nd edn., rev., Oxford, 1958, p. x).

All quotations from Jonson are from the Herford and Simpson edition (Oxford, 1925–52) and the plays are referred to as follows:

Alc.	*The Alchemist.*
B.F.	*Bartholomew Fair.*
Cat.	*Catiline His Conspiracy.*
Cyn. Rev.	*Cynthia's Revels, or The Fountain of Self-Love.*
E.M. Out	*Everyman Out of His Humour.*
Poet.	*Poetaster, or, The Arraignment.*
Sej.	*Sejanus his Fall.*

Quotations from the works of dramatists whose plays are available in a number of modern editions are referred to only by act, scene and line; where possible, Revels editions are preferred.

In Appendix B Spenser's *Works* are referred to as follows:

Amor.	*Amoretti.*
Colin	*Colin Clouts Come Home Again.*
Daph.	*Daphnaida.*
Ded. Son.	*Verses addressed by the author of The Faerie Queene to Various Noblemen.*
F. Q.	*The Faerie Queene.*
Gnat.	*Vergil's Gnat.*
Hub.	*Prosopopoia, or, Mother Hubbard's Tale.*
S.C.	*The Shepheards Calender.*

All quotations and translations from the plays and prose of Seneca (unless otherwise indicated) are derived from the Loeb editions.

To
Madeleine Kingerley

Introduction

(a) *The Quarto*. *Antonio's Revenge*, which is the second part of *Antonio and Mellida*, was entered in the Stationers' Register on 24 October 1601 by Mathew Lownes and Thomas Fisher:

> Entred for their Copye under the hande of the wardens a booke called The ffyrst and second partes of the play called Anthonio and melida provided that the gett laufull licence for yt vj^d [1]

Due licence was apparently forthcoming, for in 1602 the plays were published in Quarto, the title page of *Antonio's Revenge* affirming that '*it hath beene sundry times acted, by the children of Paules.*'[2] The halcyon device on the title page was Fisher's, and the printer was Richard Bradock.[3] While Mathew Lownes was concerned with the publication of *Antonio and Mellida*, Fisher alone appears to have been involved with *Antonio's Revenge*.

Fisher's Quarto is, on the whole, well printed, but Bradock did use a set of very badly cast punctuation marks with a full point often resembling a comma. No real attempt was made to indicate the play's many interrupted speeches, and there are several instances of mislineation, suggesting, to the Malone reprint editors[4], either carelessness on the compositor's part or that the manuscript was at times difficult to read.

In the 1602 Quarto of *Antonio and Mellida* occurs the stage direction at IV.i.29.1, *Enter Andrugio, Lucio, Cole and Norwood.* During the visitation of Bishop Bancroft to the Paul's Choir in 1598 a list of choirboys was drawn up which includes a Robert Coles and a John Norwood.[5] This Quarto, then, preserves the names of two of its original actors, which suggests that the manuscript source for the text was prompt copy. Similarly in *Antonio's Revenge* there are comparable indications of theatrical origin for the text:

> *An.* The black iades of swart night trot foggy rings
> Bout heavens browe. (12) Tis now starke
> deade night.   [III.i.1–2]

The number in parentheses directs the sounding of the chimes of midnight. Another example occurs at IV.ii.35–6;

> *Pier.* Forbeare, *Balurdo,* let the foole alone,
> Come hither (*ficto*) Is he your foole?

This seems to be a director's note that the actor should speak in an affected or incredulous tone.

Like his rival, Jonson, Marston looked upon his plays as 'Works'; he felt a responsibility to ensure the accurate transmission of what he had said. In the 1604 Quarto of *The Malcontent* he observes that he himself 'set forth this Comedie', and in 1606 two Quartos of *The Fawne* appeared, in the second of which the title page reads: 'now corrected of many faults, which by reason of the Authors absence, were let slip in the first edition'. At the same time there is a certain, perhaps affected, negligence about his attitude, an aristocratic disdain for scrupulous accuracy:

> Reader, know I have perused this coppy, to make some satisfaction for the first faulty impression; yet so urgent hath been my business, that some errors have styll passed, which thy discretion may amend.

The Quarto of *Antonio's Revenge* is, by Elizabethan standards, printed with care and accuracy: it suggests an origin in a corrected autograph manuscript which had been, at some stage, used in the actual production of the play. At the turn of the seventeenth century Marston was a leading figure in the Paul's Boys company, and it is not unlikely that he had an important share in the direction and production of his own plays. As he made no known objection to the Quarto of *Antonio's Revenge*, while he did object to inaccuracies in the first Quarto of *The Fawne* and himself corrected *The Malcontent*, Fisher's edition apparently satisfied him as to its accuracy.

(b) *Later editions.* One other edition of *Antonio's Revenge* appeared during Marston's lifetime. In 1633 William Sheares printed a

collected edition of six of Marston's plays; *Antonio and Mellida,*
Antonio's Revenge, Sophonisba, What You Will, The Fawne and
The Dutch Courtesan. This edition exists in two issues. The imprint
of the first calls the book '*The Workes of Mr. John Marston*'; the
imprint of the second reads '*Tragedies and Comedies collected into*
one volume'.[6] Brettle comments:

> It would appear that in this second issue any mention of Marston's
> name was omitted. A new general title-page was supplied; the
> publisher's preliminary epistle was left out; anonymous title-
> pages were given to the several plays; and the two signed
> dramatist's addresses to the reader were left unsigned.[7]

The Stationers' Register contains no reference to Sheares having
any rights in Marston's plays at all, and while the copy for
Antonio's Revenge was probably considered derelict, Fisher having
apparently gone out of business after 1602, that for other of the
plays was very clearly still owned.[8] Sheares, then, pirated these
plays and perhaps took the risk of publication on the assumption
that the owners of the copies might not be very anxious to claim
their rights in a period when the attack on plays and players was
approaching its apogee. In this year the Master of the Revels
ordered the re-licensing of old plays,[9] and it also saw the publication of Prynne's *Histrio-Mastix,* in a sense the summation of the
Puritan attack on the stage.

In his preliminary epistle to the first issue of the 1633 edition
Sheares makes the apology 'were it not that hee [Marston] is so
farre distant from this place, hee would have beene more carefull
in revising the former Impressions, and more circumspect about
this, then I can.' This Greg calls 'an impudent claim', for Sheares
would have us infer that he has the author's blessing for the
edition.[10] The whole tone of the preface, indeed, seems designed to
forestall criticism. Alluding to *Histrio-Mastix,* Sheares attempts
to defend plays on the facile grounds that only by the name are they
held odious; call them 'Works' and they are vindicated. He con-
tinues his apology in more specific terms, which may be addressed
to the author himself, assuring the 'grave divine' that he need not
be ashamed of his 'youthful Recreations', for

hee is free from all obscene speeches, which is the chiefe cause that makes Playes to bee so odious unto most men. Hee abhorres such Writers, and their Workes, and hath professed himselfe an enemie to all such as stuffe their Scenes with ribaldry, and lard their lines with scurrilous taunts and jests.

Marston had left the stage and entered the Church in 1609. In 1633, in view of the prevailing climate of opinion, he was probably anxious to conceal his earlier association with the drama. He may well have been in the city when he heard of Sheares's edition or, indeed, seen a copy of the first issue, for we know that he died in London in 1634. Editorially Marston was unlikely to be flattered by Sheares's edition, for its text of *The Fawne* omitted the author's corrections in Q2. The probable explanation for the cancels in the second issue of the 1633 edition is thus that Marston personally objected to its printing. There is no reason to suppose that it was the owners of the copies who objected, as they would hardly have been satisfied with the mere substitution of cancels for the first-issue title-leaves. In the second issue of the 1633 edition the intention was to remove all traces of authorship; in fact few extant copies contain a complete set of cancels.

The play's text in the 1633 edition, first issue, is a reprint of the Quarto with the correction of a few obvious errors, but there is no evidence to suggest that the copy was corrected by reference to an independent manuscript source. The second issue, 1633, is a reprint of the first, with variations in the use of italic and roman type. Sheares's edition is an unethical, unintelligent stationer's reprint.

The only other seventeenth-century reference to an edition of Marston's plays occurs in the *Remains of Sr. Walter Raleigh: printed for Henry Mortlock* (London, 1675), where the publisher's advertisement includes, among thirty other items, 'Mr. *John Marston's six Playes, in 8vo.*'; perhaps Mortlock acquired the remainder of Sheares's stock.

Antonio's Revenge has been infrequently reprinted in modern times, but it does appear in the following editions and reprints:

The Works of John Marston, ed. J. O. Halliwell (London, 1856), I, 69–144.

The Works of the British Dramatists, ed. J. S. Keltie (Edinburgh, 1872), 364–82.

The Works of John Marston, ed. A. H. Bullen (London, 1887), I, 95–191.

Antonio and Mellida and Antonio's Revenge, ed. W. W. Greg (1602; facsimile rpt. London: Malone Society, 1921).

The Plays of John Marston, ed. H. H. Wood (Edinburgh, 1934), I, 65–133.

Antonio's Revenge, ed. G. K. Hunter (Lincoln, Nebraska: Regents Renaissance Drama, 1965).

In Halliwell's edition no line numbering was attempted and the act and scene divisions were left as in the Quarto; Keltie began a tradition of redividing the scenes into larger units and Bullen followed suit; Wood reverts to the Quarto divisions without line numbers; Hunter uses the larger scene-units and adds line numbers.

(c) *This edition.* The present edition is based upon a collation of all copies of the Quarto of 1602 known to me:[11] I have found no corrections in proof.[12] I have adopted the Quarto divisions of act and scene, as they are probably authorial, and, as the Quarto is used as the exclusive copy text, departures from it are recorded in the collation or annotation. All subsequent texts have been treated as editions, and their departures from the Quarto are collated only when and if they suggest a substantial and plausible verbal or sense change to the copy text. No attempt has been made to provide a variorum collation, and minor variations in spelling and punctuation are ignored: from the Quarto, foul case and turned letters are silently corrected. In accordance with the practice of this series the spelling has been modernised. One of the features of Marston's writing is his habit of either coining new words or phrases or using expressions in new senses; I have, therefore, as far as possible, tried to include in the collation the Quarto spelling of these Marston originals—when their seventeenth-century and modern forms differ. I am not, of course, implying by this practice that all the spellings in the Quarto are authorial; there is no accurate means of determining the degree of compositorial interference but, as the manuscript used for setting up the Quarto was probably a corrected autograph, there is a high probability, especially in the case of new or unusual words, that their form originated with Marston.

The punctuation of the text, which is the most careless aspect of the Quarto's printing, has been altered to conform to modern practice. I do not mean by this an attempt at 'dramatic pointing', for I am unconvinced that we know enough about either acting methods or punctuation habits in the seventeenth century to be able to recapture the rhetorical impact of the original performance. I have, however, attempted to refrain from the use of punctuation marks wherever possible so as not to interfere with the free flow of the speeches. I have, on the whole, used lighter punctuation than that of the Quarto.

The stage directions are almost all provided by the Quarto, but in a few cases I have felt it necessary to add others. This has been done on the assumption that the chances of the reader being able to attend a performance of this play, except imaginatively, are remote.

Although he is a hostile critic, Ben Jonson makes it clear that *Antonio's Revenge* astonished the theatre-going public of early seventeenth-century London. One reason for their surprise appears to have been Marston's choice of dramatic language. This is the justification for the departure from normal Revels practice in the commentary to this edition of the play. An asterisk will frequently be found after the lemma: it is designed to indicate a word the usage of which seems to have been initiated, at least on the stage and in print, by Marston in this play. I hope that this visual indication of the extent of Marston's verbal invention will help to recapture something of the effect of the original performances.

2. JOHN MARSTON

John Marston[13] was of mainly English ancestry; his father, also John, of the Middle Temple, was of an old Shropshire family, but his mother, Marie, was the daughter of an Italian surgeon, Andrew Guarsi, whose family had become resident in London during the reign of Henry VIII. Their only child was baptised at Wardington, Oxfordshire, on 7 October 1576. The family probably moved to Coventry shortly after the christening.[14]

Marston received his university education at Brasenose College, Oxford, where he was in residence from 1591, although he did not matriculate until 4 February in the following year, when he became sixteen. When he graduated B.A. on 23 March 1594 he had already been admitted to the Middle Temple (on 2 August 1592). He is not, however, known to have resided in London before November 1595. From June 1597 he shared his father's chambers, but his interests were literary as well as legal, for on 27 May 1598 *The Metamorphosis of Pigmalions Image and Certain Satyres* was listed in the Stationers' Register. This contained an erotic Ovidian love poem and five satires, one of which, *Reactio*, attacked Joseph Hall, the author of *Virgidemiarum, Sixe Bookes* (registered 31 March 1597), also a work of satire.[15] This attack is continued by Marston in his second book of satires, *The Scourge of Villanie* (registered 8 September 1598). In the second edition of this latter work, *Satyra Nova* is devoted to attacking Hall and is addressed to E.G., probably Everard Guilpin, author of *Skialetheia* (1598), who was a member of Gray's Inn and had been a member of Hall's college at Cambridge, Emmanuel. Guilpin and Marston were both young men seeking to make a name in the new, fashionable mode of formal satire;[16] the attack on Hall may have been motivated as much by acrimony as by a desire to create gossip. By Christmas of this same year Marston had probably turned dramatist, producing *Histriomastix*, an old-style morality play with a legal theme and much legal phraseology, for the Christmas Revels at the Middle Temple.[17]

Within six months he was notorious. On 1 June 1599 Archbishop Whitgift of Canterbury and Bishop Bancroft of London commanded the destruction of sundry satirical and otherwise offensive publications: *Pygmalion* and *The Scourge* were burnt by the common hangman. Three months later, on 28 September, Henslowe, treasurer for the Admiral's Men, paid £2 to William Bourne as a loan to 'mr maxton the new poete in earneste of a Boocke':[18] the book was perhaps the lost play *The King of Scots*, a collaborative effort of Marston, Chettle, Dekker and Jonson.[19]

Marston's father died later this same year and his will (proved 29 November) bears witness to his son's preoccupation:

> To s[ai]d son John my furniture etc. in my chambers in the Middle Temple my law books etc. to my s[ai]d son whom I hoped would have profited by them in the study of the law but man proposeth and God disposeth etc.

Marston's literary aspirations may have been encouraged by his inheritance, which was probably substantial;[20] certainly his father was aware that a legal career for his son was improbable.

The single entry in Henslowe's diary is Marston's only known association with the professional adult stage, and his next literary production, the satiric romance *Antonio and Mellida* (late 1599), was produced for and performed by the Paul's Boys. From mid-May 1599 the Paul's choir was under the mastership of Edward Pearce, and their revival as an acting company was financed by William Stanley (sixth Earl of Derby), an amateur playwright and a member of Lincoln's Inn. The revival at Paul's saw the first performances by boy players in London for nine years. Probably Marston abandoned his brief association with the professional stage as soon as the opportunity arose to be involved with this revived fashion in the more aristocratic company of a private boys' theatre, and he remained with the Paul's company for the next three years.

Coincident with the progress of his role as dramatist of Paul's, Marston became involved in a second literary quarrel; this time the man attacked was Ben Jonson, but larger rivalries were also concerned, for the dispute became a contention about literary taste and a trial of public popularity between adult and boy theatres. This was the notorious Poetomachia,[21] about which Jonson later boasted to Drummond,

> he had many quarrells with Marston beat him and took his Pistol from him, wrote his Poetaster on him the beginning of them were that Marston represented him in the stage.[22]

The Induction to *Antonio and Mellida* promises that, if it is successful, there will be a second part—this is *Antonio's Revenge* (probably late 1600 or early 1601), and it was some of the stylistic and linguistic idiosyncrasies of this play that Jonson later singled out for special vituperation. Partially as a result of the interest created by the Poetomachia, Marston was a success as a private theatre dramatist, and the Paul's Boys proved a popular attraction, as the setting up of the rival Chapel Children at the Blackfriars attests. Marston contributed two other plays to Paul's during this first intense period of activity and rivalry, *Jack Drum's Entertainment* (*c.* 1600), a domestic comedy which was perhaps a revision of an older play, and *What You Will* (1601), a romantic comedy with a strong satirical content.[23]

Marston was by this time considered a poet of major standing, at least by his fellow member of the Middle Temple, Sir John Salusbury of Lleweni, for he was invited along with Shakespeare, Chapman and Jonson (despite the concurrent public-personal dispute) to contribute to a volume in honour of Sir John's recently acquired knighthood. This was *Love's Martyr* (1601) by Robert Chester, and Marston's contribution suggests an intimate acquaintance with the Salusbury family.[24] He was, however, also in this year in difficulties in the Middle Temple, for on 14 October he was expelled from his rooms for non-payment of dues and non-residence in the preceding half-year. On 27 November he was restored to his former standing but not to his chambers.

While 1601 probably represents the year when his contemporary literary fame was at its height, it was also the year of his sensational and damning public humiliation. In Jonson's *Poetaster* Marston, in the person of Crispinus, was forced to vomit up in public his new-coined words and fashionable jargon. Perhaps his long absence from the Middle Temple during this year may be accounted for by his withdrawal from his usual haunts, until he could find a way to recover his lost personal and dramatic dignity. Whatever the explanation, there now occurs a two-year hiatus in Marston's literary career, and his next play, *The Dutch Courtesan*, an outspokenly satiric comedy, was probably performed in late 1603 or early 1604, but not by the Paul's Boys.[25] Some time subsequent to his humiliation in *Poetaster* Marston transferred his allegiance to the Children of the Queen's Revels (formerly the Chapel Children) at the Blackfriars and acquired a one-sixth share in the company. For the Blackfriars syndicate Marston wrote his most celebrated play, *The Malcontent* (1604?), which was later performed by the King's Men with additions by John Webster. Marston had, by this time, re-established cordial relations with Jonson, for *The Malcontent* is handsomely dedicated to 'Beniamino Jonsonio, poetae elegantissimo . . . amico suo', and he had written gratulatory verses for Jonson's *Sejanus* (1603).

In late 1604 or early 1605 Marston produced another satiric comedy, *The Fawne*, which was 'divers times presented at the blacke Friars'. In this latter year too it seems that he was married to Mary, daughter of Dr William Wilkes, rector of Barford St Martins in Wiltshire. At this time he was enjoying a substantial contemporary reputation, for William Camden, the foremost Elizabethan antiquary, includes Marston in the company of Spenser, Sidney, Daniel, Holland, Jonson, Campion, Drayton, Chapman and Shakespeare in his *Remaines of a Greater Worke, concerning Britaine* (1605). He lists these poets as the 'most pregnant witts of these our times, whom succeeding ages may iustly admire'.[26]

Marston's new-found cordiality with Jonson caused the first months of his married life to be distinctly anxious ones, for he collaborated with him and with Chapman on *Eastward Ho!*, which proved highly objectionable to James I. The play made contemptuous reference to the Scots, and Sir James Murray reported the facts to the King; the result, according to Drummond, was that Jonson 'voluntarily imprissoned himself with Chapman and Marston'. Marston's collaborators seem to have tried to put the whole blame for the offensive remarks on him. For a time there was a danger lest 'they should then [have] had their ears cut and noses', but they were pardoned and freed by November.[27] The anger which this incident aroused probably accounts for Marston's sneer in his preface to his next play, a tragedy, *Sophonisba* (1606):

> To transcribe Authors, quote authorities, and translate Latin prose orations into English blank-verse, hath in this subject beene the least aime of my studies.

Jonson's *Sejanus* is a fairly obvious target.

Despite the offence of *Eastward Ho!*, or perhaps by way of

apology for it, we find Marston providing a Latin pageant for the royal welcome accorded King Christian IV of Denmark to London on 31 July 1606. In the following year he wrote *An Entertainment*, which was performed at Ashby, for Alice, Countess Dowager of Derby, and in August, writing to Sir Gervase Clifton and probably referring to this entertainment, he apologises for the delay in sending copies of the text, 'for all the rest which I had caused to be transcribed were given and stolen from me att my Lord Spencer's [Baron Spencer of Wormleighton]'.[28] His works were still in demand.

The next surviving official notice of Marston occurs on 8 June 1608, when he was committed to Newgate.[29] The nature of the offence is not known, but it may have been some further satirical dramatic indiscretion in a lost play similar to that in *Eastward Ho!*. This imprisonment may explain why after this time, and leaving his last play, *The Insatiate Countess*, incomplete (although later additions were made by William Barksted), Marston turned from the theatre to the Church. By early 1610 'Marston the poet' was preaching at Oxford.[30]

On 24 September 1609 he had been ordained deacon in the parish church of Stanton Harcourt in Oxfordshire; soon afterwards he was accepted as a student at St Mary Hall; on 29 December he was made priest.[31] Some three weeks before his ordination Marston had applied for permission to read in the Bodleian Library, affirming that he had been studying philosophy for three years. His conversion from stage to pulpit perhaps began in 1606. On 18 June 1610 he describes himself, when witnessing a legal document, as 'of Barford in the county of Wilts clerk'. This suggests that he was living with his father-in-law William Wilkes, incumbent of Barford. In his will, dated 6 May 1630, and referring to a period prior to 1616, Wilkes forgives Marston 'al that is or may bee due unto mee for lodging and diet, for himselfe, his wife, his man, and mayde which he had of me for eleaven yeares'. Marston may have fled to Barford during the *Eastward Ho!* troubles, and if so it helps to explain Jonson's jeer to Drummond,

Marston wrott his Father in Lawes preachings and his Father in Law his Commedies.[32]

Although living in Wiltshire Marston, at least occasionally, visited the London area, for he was the victim of a highway robbery at the hands of Sir George Sandys in August 1616 near Knightsbridge in Essex. On 10 October of this same year he was presented to the curacy of Christchurch in Hampshire, which he retained until 13 September 1631. His only son, also John, died an infant in 1624.

In 1633 William Sheares published his unauthorised edition of some of Marston's plays, dedicated to Elizabeth Cary, Viscountess Falkland. In his Preface Sheares speaks of the author as being 'in his Autumne and declining age' but Marston was vigorous enough to object strenuously to the edition.[33] He died in London on 25 June 1634 and was buried beside his father in the Temple Church; his tombstone was inscribed 'Oblivioni Sacrum'. A fitter contemporary epitaph might have been the words of Antony à Wood,

> [he] was not inferior to any in writing of comedies and tragedies, especially if you consider the time when they were penn'd; and perhaps equal to some who lived 20 yeares after his time.[34]

3. DATE AND SOURCES

Antonio's Revenge, together with its first part, *Antonio and Mellida*, was entered in the Stationers' Register on 24 October 1601; it is highly improbable that it was written before 1599. The attempt to establish its date of composition and production more precisely within these limits is, however, a matter of continuing controversy, because the dating of this play is inextricably involved with the problem of the date of Shakespeare's *Hamlet*.

There are three major theories to explain the relationship between Marston's play and Shakespeare's; the first of these argues that *Antonio's Revenge* precedes *Hamlet*. In *Antonio and Mellida*, v.i, a painter shows Balurdo two portraits, one inscribed '*Anno Domini 1599*' and the other '*Aetatis suae 24*'; it has been assumed that the first date refers to the year of production and the second to the age of the author. The Prologue to *Antonio's Revenge* refers to a change of season from summer to early winter when 'drizzling sleet' (2), and 'snarling gusts nibble the juiceless leaves' (4). Before 1927, when R. E. Brettle discovered that Marston was

christened on 7 October 1576,[35] the available evidence suggested
that he was born in 1575; thus E. K. Chambers could assert with
some confidence,

> As he [Marston] must have completed his twenty-fourth year by
> 3 February 1600 at latest, Part i [*Ant. & Mel.*] was probably
> produced in 1599. The Prologue of Part ii [*Ant. Rev.*] speaks of
> winter as replacing summer, and probably Part i is to be dated in
> the summer, and Part ii in the early winter of 1599.[36]

But since Brettle's discovery this conclusion no longer holds—
Marston was probably born in late September or early October
1576. Some critics since then, among them D. J. McGinn,
have argued that as 'he would have become twenty-four years
of age not earlier than the fall of 1600 . . . the inscriptions on
the pictures present little or no biographical information'.[37] This
objection to the discrepancy in the age twenty-four of the portrait
and Marston's actual twenty-three years has been used to add
factual weight to the subjective feeling that '*Antonio's Revenge*
reeks of *Hamlet* and it reeks of theft'.[38] According to the second
theory, then, *Antonio's Revenge* is wholly derivative from *Hamlet*.

The third theory seeks to effect a compromise,[39] and argues that
there are no conclusive grounds on which to establish the prece-
dence of either Marston's play or Shakespeare's: a conclusion
with which I would concur. Smith, Pizer and Kaufman point out
that Marston was in his twenty-fourth year in 1599 and argue that
Shakespeare and Marston were working at the same time and in
competition on a revenge play, 'neither able to see what the other
was doing, each with an eye on the old Hamlet play', i.e. the
posited *Ur-Hamlet*.[40]

Advocates of all three of these theories agree, at least, that the
similarities between *Antonio's Revenge* and *Hamlet* cannot be
explained by pure coincidence: they either derive the one from the
other or from a common original. Secondly, they all feel that
Shakespeare and Marston, writing respectively for the adult and
boy players, were in competition to attract custom.

Antonio's Revenge was originally intended as a sequel to *Antonio
and Mellida*, for Antonio in the 'Induction' to the earlier play
observes,

I have heard that those persons, as he [i.e. Galeatzo] and you, Feliche, that are but slightly drawn in this comedy, should receive more exact accomplishment in a second part; which, if this obtain gracious acceptance, means to try his fortune. [134–8]

In the 'second part', however, Feliche appears only as a corpse, and the sequel is a tragedy of blood and not a recapitulation of the 'comic crosses of true love' (v.ii.264). This discrepancy between original intent and execution perhaps implies a reasonable interval between the two parts. There seems to me to be no reason to discredit the date 1599 offered in *Antonio and Mellida* for that play; but Marston is using old-style dating, whereby the year ends on 24 March, so that the play could be as late as March 1600, according to the modern calendar.

Antonio's Revenge preceded Jonson's *Poetaster*, and *Poetaster* was dated 1601 by Jonson in the Folio of 1616; it was probably performed not later than May.[41] In *Poetaster*, *Antonio's Revenge* seems to be an especial object of Jonson's acrimony. He parodies the line 'The fist of strenuous Vengeance is clutched' (*Ant. Rev.*, v.i.3) by mocking Marston's use of the word 'vengeance' as a trisyllable: 'Of strenuous venge-ance to clutch the fist' (*Poet.*, v.iii.292). Jonson also speaks sarcastically of 'cothurnall buskins' (*Poet.*, v.iii.281), a reference to the line 'O now *Tragoedia Cothurnata* mounts' (*Ant. Rev.*, II.v.45). Similarly, when he sneers at Marston's use of the word 'incubus', he is probably thinking of the metaphorical usage by Strotzo,

> I would have told you, if the incubus
> That rides your bosom would have patience.
> [*Ant. Rev.*, I.i.90–1]

Jonson causes Crispinus (one of the poetasters of the title) to vomit up, among others, the words 'clumsy' (*Ant. Rev.*, Prol. 1), 'strenuous' (*Ant. Rev.*, v.i.3), 'clutched' (*Ant. Rev.*, I.i.3), and 'snarling gusts' (*Ant. Rev.*, Prol., 4). Crispinus is Marston, but Jonson's virulent attack on his diction depends for its effect on the recognition by the audience of the quotations from Marston's work, with *Antonio's Revenge* as the primary example. It thus seems safe to infer that, at the time of the production of *Poetaster*,

Antonio's Revenge was either currently being played at Paul's or had just recently been played there. The available evidence makes a date for the production of *Antonio's Revenge* in the winter of 1600–01 the most likely conclusion.[42]

I have already indicated my preference for the view that Marston used the same source for *Antonio's Revenge* as Shakespeare did for *Hamlet*, rather than either play deriving from the other. Before examining this common source, however, it is pertinent to consider the roles of both Shakespeare's company, the Lord Chamberlain's Men, and Marston's, the Children of Paul's, in the War of the Theatres or Poetomachia. Allusion has been made to the personal dispute between Jonson and Marston in 1600–01 which led to Jonson's attack on Marston's diction in his *Poetaster*. Their personal battle—which evidently involved them only as playwrights, for at the very time they both, like Shakespeare, contributed to Chester's *Loves Martyr*—was part of a more complex pattern of theatrical rivalry. This competition between theatres arose from the sudden immense success of the Children of the Chapel at the Blackfriars at the turn of the seventeenth century, for their popularity was so great that they threatened the livelihood of the adult London companies. In *Hamlet* Rosencrantz alludes to this situation in the famous passage on 'an aery of children, little eyeases' (II.ii.342). The clearer reference in the Q1 text bears citing:

> For the principall publike audience that
> Came to them, are turned to private playes,
> And to the humour of children.   [*sig.* E2*v*]

While Shakespeare confined himself to this brief allusion, his company evidently hired Thomas Dekker to make a more direct attack on Ben Jonson, who at this time was writing for the Children of Blackfriars. This came to Jonson's notice, and he responded with the quick composition of *Poetaster* in 1601, in which he attacked not only Marston in the character of Crispinus but also Dekker as the poetaster Demetrius. In III.iv Histrio, who represents a company of adult players, refers to Dekker:

> we have hired him to abuse Horace [i.e. Jonson], and bring him in, in a play, with all his gallants ...

And shortly after he laments:

> this winter ha's made us all poorer, then so many starv'd snakes:
> No bodie comes to us; not a gentleman . . .   [321–2, 328–9]

Jonson is jeering at the adult players' lack of success.

Dekker replied rather weakly, later in 1601, in *Satiromastix*. What is significant for our purposes is that this play was first acted at the Globe by Shakespeare's company and then also at Paul's, while *Poetaster*—which attacks both Dekker and Marston—was acted only at Blackfriars. There was evidently, then, some collaboration in 1601 between the boys of Paul's and the men of the Globe against a common rival, the boys of Blackfriars. And indeed the Lord Chamberlain's Men had little need to be troubled by the boys of Paul's, who sought an audience of quality in a small playhouse.[43] The Blackfriars, on the other hand, could seat 'several hundred persons', and it was therefore the Children of the Chapel who offered 'damaging competition' to the Globe.[44] It is noteworthy that Rosencrantz speaks of 'an aery of children', one competitor.

Turning now to the relation between *Antonio's Revenge* and *Hamlet*, they have many similarities of plot, incident and character, but no exact verbal parallels,[45] though both include precise verbal echoes from *The Spanish Tragedy*. Neither Shakespeare nor Marston would seem to have had access to the other's text, but, given the collaboration in 1601 of Paul's and the Globe and the fact that the Children of the Chapel were their common enemies, it is possible that each dramatist was aware of what the other was doing. The two theatres may have agreed to co-operate on a play of a similar kind, written, however, from the different viewpoints of boy and adult actor, to form a united challenge to their common rival, the Children of the Chapel. This co-operation without collaboration might help to explain the very close likeness of plot in the two plays but the absence of identical phrasing. *Antonio's Revenge* and *Hamlet* were written contemporaneously, the plot and major outlines of the characters were shared, but the treatment remained each dramatist's own.

The principal source for both plays, then, was probably a lost play on the Hamlet theme (the so-called *Ur-Hamlet*) which had been played by 1596, since Thomas Lodge in *Wits Miserie* speaks, in that year, of

> a foule lubber, his tongue tipt with lying, his heart steeld against charity, he walks for the most part in black under colour of gravity, and looks as pale as the Visard of the ghost which cried so miserally at the Theator like an oisterwife, Hamlet, revenge . . .
>
> [*sig.* h.iiiiv, *unsigned*]

It may have existed as early as 1589, when Thomas Nashe spoke of 'whole Hamlets . . . handfuls of Tragicall speeches'.[46] The *Ur-Hamlet* was probably Senecan in tone and was perhaps written by Thomas Kyd, but what precise interpretation and what exact details it gave to the Hamlet story remain a matter of pure conjecture.[47]

As a tale Hamlet's fate was recounted by Saxo Grammaticus, the twelfth-century Danish historian, in his *Historia Danica* and later by François de Belleforest as one of his *Histoires Tragiques* (1571) [Book v, pp. 197–302], which was translated into English as *The Historie of Hamblet*.[48] No edition of this translation can, however, be traced before 1608, and I agree with Elze[49] that *Hamblet* is probably 'the book of the play'. The author of the *Ur-Hamlet*, as well as Shakespeare and Marston, could have been familiar with Belleforest's French original, which

> is a primitive tale of lust, blood-feuds and revenge. It embraces the marriage of Horvvendille, governor of Diethmarsen, with Geruthe, daughter of the King of Denmark, and the birth of their son Amleth; the murder of Horvvendille by his brother Fengon, and the latter's union with Geruthe, whom he had previously seduced; Amleth's pretense of madness to compass his revenge on his uncle; his interview with his mother in a closet, and the murder of an eaves-dropping councillor; his dispatch by Fengon to England with secret instructions for his assassination; his discovery of the plot and return, followed by the execution of his long-delayed vengeance; his ascent afterwards of the Danish throne, his double marriage, and his death in battle at the hands of his maternal uncle Wiglere.[50]

Belleforest's account is a substantially accurate rendering of Grammaticus' Latin original, with the exception that Grammaticus says nothing of an adulterous liaison between Feng and Gerutha before Horwendil's death and that Feng argues that Gerutha 'had been visited with her husband's extremest hate; and it was all to save her that he had slain his brother'.[51] These two versions of this tale are, then, in all probability the source for all three Hamlet plays.

In the case of Shakespeare's and Marston's plays, however, there are similarities between them derived neither from Grammaticus nor from Belleforest. In both *Antonio's Revenge* and *Hamlet*

> the ghost of the victim appears at midnight to tell his child the true circumstances of his death and to demand revenge. . . . [Both revengers] suspect their mothers of complicity and are tempted to desire their deaths, but the ghost in either play though grieved at his wife's falling-off takes a more charitable view, and on his second appearance (in his wife's chamber with both wife and son present) commands that the son comfort his mother or rather, in the case of Andrugio, undertakes that office himself, having persuaded her to repentance.[52]

On at least one occasion both ghosts speak from beneath the stage to urge on the vengeance, and both revengers hold back on the first opportunity to slay their adversary.

These correspondences are presumably to be explained by their common origin in the lost *Ur-Hamlet* and the possible co-operation between Shakespeare and Marston in the development of their plays. *Antonio's Revenge* and *Hamlet* are directly comparable in terms of incident and character, but the style and language of their composition remain, distinctively, each dramatist's own.

Marston treats the Hamlet story with ironic melodrama, sensation and a marked preference for ingenuity of torment; *Antonio's Revenge* is a blood-feud. He borrows Shakespeare's famous wooing of a heroine by a villain from *Richard the Third*, when Piero woos Maria, whose husband, Andrugio, he has slain, and possibly derives some of the tortures of Piero in the concluding masque-of-revenge, when Piero's tongue is torn out by the avengers, from the indignities suffered by Lavinia in *Titus Andronicus*. His imagination is also often stimulated by the lurid and bloody incidents of Senecan tragedy. Antonio cites Seneca's *Thyestes* and his *Aga-*

memnon with unfeigned admiration, and Pandulpho adopts a Stoic manner of emotional reticence. Similarly Marston owes a debt to Kyd's *Spanish Tragedy*, not merely when he cites its dialogue but for the machinery of revenge and its atmosphere: like Horatio, son of Hieronimo, Feliche's body is discovered hung 'in an arbour', and Antonio, like Hieronimo, digs into the stage with his dagger in a frenzy of revengeful passion. This density of literary allusion in *Antonio's Revenge* is surely deliberate; it suggests that this particular play is only one example of a tradition greater and more enduring than it.

As Marston's essential dramatic inspiration is Senecan, so is his philosophical inspiration. Both Pandulpho and Antonio cite with approval the sentiments of the *De Providentia*, and both of them as well as Maria make extensive use of the translation by Whyttynton of the *De Remediis Fortuitorum*. In Act IV, scene v, the speeches of Antonio and Pandulpho substantially consist of quotations from and allusions to this particular piece of Senecan moralising. Whyttynton's translation of the *De Remediis* ranks as Marston's primary specifically identified source.[53]

Whether or not there was collusion between Marston and Shakespeare in the production of their two plays on the 'Amleth' theme, Marston's contribution tends always to be overshadowed for us by Shakespeare's. While there is no doubt that Marston owed a considerable debt to the *Ur-Hamlet* tradition, Shakespeare's obligation was perhaps no less heavy, and *Antonio's Revenge* is, in its unique way, a successful product for the theatre of the boys which utilises effects and devices available, at that time, only to them.

4. THE PLAY AND ITS CRITICS

The literary criticism of *Antonio's Revenge* begins with Ben Jonson, In *Poetaster* Jonson condemns the style as 'barren trash' (v.iii.373) and calls its author a 'ierking pedant' (v.iii.371), a mere '*prettie stoick*' (III.i.28). While his attack on Marston is mere abuse, Jonson's critical condemnation of the play was highly successful, for its rehabilitation was not attempted for some two centuries.

In 1808, in his *Specimens of English Dramatic Poets*, Charles Lamb praised the Prologue, declaring that

for its passionate earnestness, and for the tragic note of prepara-
tion which it sounds . . . It is as solemn a preparative as the
'warning voice which he who saw the Apocalypse, heard cry'.[54]

But this judgement is, in its own way, as extreme as Jonson's, and
the modern assessment was more nearly approached by Swin-
burne:

> A vehement and resolute desire to give weight to every line and
> emphasis to every phrase has too often misled him into such
> brakes and jungles of crabbed and convulsive bombast, of stiff
> and tortuous exhuberance that the reader in struggling through
> some of the scenes and speeches feels as though he were com-
> pelled to push his way through a cactus hedge.[55]

In the early 1930s Theodore Spencer pointed out that the trouble
with Marston's style is that

> he tries to force individual words to do more than they have any
> business to, and worse still, he usually chooses the wrong words
> for his purpose. He experiments continually with rhythms and
> unusual words, but, since he had little instinctive taste, or sense
> of what makes poetry 'right', the experiments nearly always fail.

Nevertheless he still found in him a foreshadowing of the metaphysical style and felt that Marston's atrocities of diction at least
taught his fellow poets what to avoid.[56] Una Ellis-Fermor takes this
argument a step further by pointing out that his fantastic diction
is part of a deliberate theatrical effect, and suggests that in the
characters of Piero and Balurdo, with their numerous broken
speeches, Marston was attempting to capture the actual idiom of
speech more accurately than had been achieved by his contemporaries.[57]

It can hardly be denied that Marston suffers, especially in
Antonio's Revenge, from linguistic indigestion, but Jonson did not
understand Marston's stylistic habits. Out of 327 words explained
in the commentary to this edition (and listed in Appendix B),
Shakespeare uses 62 per cent, Spenser 38 per cent, and Marston is
the first recorded user of some 26 per cent:[58] Jonson mocks a small
fraction, 7 per cent. In the broad sense of attitude towards language
Shakespeare, Spenser and Marston were on the same side, and for
all the accuracy of Jonson's detailed strictures—since Marston did

delight in cacophony for its own sake, to surprise and shock, and was often unaware of his own disharmony—this is formidable opposition. At the root of the disagreement is a basic difference of attitude towards the use of words: Jonson favoured succinctness and precision of statement at the expense of connotation, while Marston sought, on the whole, to use words for their emotive and suggestive effect.

Marston seems to have made it a particular mark of his style to use as many newly coined words and phrases (originating a very large proportion of these himself) as possible: Jonson, with his preference for established usage, was probably shocked at this 'vulgarisation' of the language of the drama. In *Antonio's Revenge* Marston may have been attempting to become the leading fashionable innovator in the speech habits of a socially prominent section of London society. It is true, however, that he is not able to achieve the poetic shock of the metaphysical style at its best, for we are conscious that he is deliberately choosing his words to surprise us; there is no sense that Marston's coinages are formed by the compulsion of his thought.

As F. L. Lucas points out, however, if exaggeration is the source of Marston's failures it is also, paradoxically, the reason for his successes, for

> If he owes Seneca some of his worst crudities, he owes him too some of his finest speeches in the purple vein of Renaissance individualism . . . his Senecan defiances of doom, brave words of broken men, can wake some living echoes still.[59]

It is perhaps in its moods of fatalistic despondency that Marston's verse reaches the greatest moments of Jacobean dramatic despair, as when Piero indicts the race of man

> There glow no sparks of reason in the world,
> All are raked up in ashy beastliness;
> The bulk of man's as dark as Erebus,
> No branch of reason's light hangs in his trunk;
> There lives no reason to keep league withall.   [I.iv.23–7]

While *Antonio's Revenge* may be linguistically distinctive, it is thematically conventional. It belongs to that genre defined by A. H. Thorndike as

a distinct species of the tragedy of blood . . . a tragedy whose
leading motive is revenge and whose main action deals with the
progress of this revenge, leading to the death of the murderers
and often the death of the avenger himself.[60]

It adheres rigidly to this form of revenge tragedy. But *Antonio's
Revenge* is exceptional in that it is ostensibly the second part of a
play which began as a comedy. In addition, as Fredson Bowers
points out,[61] Marston's villain is a Renaissance Italian despot and
is initially more plausible, because less of a caricature, than
Marlowe's Barabas or Shakespeare's Aaron; Piero is a portrait of
the Elizabethan notion of Machiavelli.

From the moment of his first entry *'unbraced'*, *'smeared in blood,
a poniard in one hand, bloody* . . . STROTZO *following him with a
cord'* (I.i.0.1–3), Piero is characterised by brutality and violence.
As a sadistic tyrant he is consistent, but there are elements in his
character which are difficult to absorb. We learn that Piero is not
merely a bloodthirsty villain but also a jealous and disappointed
lover; he caused the death of Andrugio because

> We both were rivals in our May of blood
> Unto Maria, fair Ferrara's heir.
> He won the Lady, to my honour's death,
> And from her sweets cropped this Antonio;
> For which I burned in inward swelt'ring hate,
> And festered rankling malice in my breast,
> Till I might belk revenge upon his eyes.   [I.i.23–9]

This is possible, but implausible: Piero, in his love-lorn character,
appears to be a device of the plot. Gradually he 'becomes a mere
hobgoblin to frighten children',[61] plotting like a caricature of
Milton's Satan to overthrow all the world,

> I'll conquer Rome,
> Pop out the light of bright religion.   [IV.iii.142–3]

Piero does not simply become deranged by power and ambition, it
is Marston who over-draws him as a fiendish Machiavel until he
becomes merely ludicrous. P. J. Finkelpearl, however, finds that
Piero remains both 'farcical' and 'lethal'.[62]

In proportion as Piero's tyranny is diabolical, so Antonio's
revenge must be fiendish. Antonio is almost Piero's peer in the

invention of ingenious torment; he slaughters Julio as a gratuitous act of horror; he conducts the macabre masque-of-avengers who tear out Piero's tongue, serve him a fricassée of Julio, and then delay the *coup de grâce* so that he may suffer as long as possible. As an avenger Antonio has little psychological depth, and yet, paradoxically, his characterisation reflects Marston's growing interest in psychology. As Hardin Craig points out, many of Antonio's speeches are concerned with an analysis of the physiology of grief.[63] He tells Alberto that his 'moist entrails' are 'crumpled up with grief' and that his heart spurs his 'gallèd ribs' with 'punching anguish' (i.v.43–5); he declares

> That grief is wanton-sick
> Whose stomach can digest and brook the diet
> Of stale ill-relished counsel. [II.iii.2–4]

Examples of this clinical interest abound. They foreshadow the study of melancholia in Malevole of *The Malcontent*.

The unrestrained violence, both physical and emotional, of Piero and Antonio—they both commit murder on stage in full view of the audience—is counterbalanced by the extreme Stoic fortitude of Pandulpho Feliche. Marston perhaps intended the Stoic calm of Pandulpho as a moderating influence amid the violence of the main action; he acts as a commentator on human misery and has, more clearly and reasonably than Antonio, a just cause for revenge. Fredson Bowers remarks that Piero's fatal error lies in underestimating Pandulpho.[64] For Una Ellis-Fermor Pandulpho has a depth which saves him from the 'mechanical inhumanity'[65] of the other characters. Pandulpho is aware that it is not in the absence of passion but in the ability to feel beyond passion that true Stoicism subsists;

> I spake more than a god,
> Yet am less than a man.
> I am the miserablest soul that breathes. [IV.v.51–3]

At times during the course of the action of the play the attitude of characters towards Stoic moral doctrine appears to amount to an uncritical adulation; yet this admiration is ambivalent. When Maria cites the objections of the *De Remediis* to feminine duplicity

(I.ii.47 ff.), she speaks entirely in character, and no ironic intent may be assumed. On the other hand, Pandulpho (altogether more credible as a person) first surprises Alberto by refusing to display grief over the murder of Feliche, then admits that 'Man will break out, despite philosophy' (IV.v.46) but proceeds to bury his son with a funeral oration derived, almost word for word, from the *De Remediis*; the oration concluded, he initiates the bloody vengeance upon Piero (IV.v.91–3). This structure of action is surely a deliberately exploited contrast between the sentiments adopted from the moral discourses of the Stoics and the actuality of the emotional conflicts in the pattern of revenge tragedy. Pandulpho is a Stoic by rational choice but a bloody avenger by emotional compulsion. Thus G. D. Aggeler asserts that the central theme of the play is 'the total moral abandonment which inevitably follows the surrender of reason to passion', for

> the villainous triumphs of Piero bring about a compulsion to revenge which reduces all of the other principal characters to his moral stature. Revenge becomes a *raison d'être* for all of them. It becomes a channel for Antonio's overpowering emotions and a substitute for the moral purposes of Pandulpho and Alberto.[66]

Antonio is quicker and more obvious than Pandulpho in his impatience with Stoicism, dismissing a quotation he reads from the *De Providentia* (II.iii.45–8) as being unacceptable as a directive in an actual human situation. Marston also seems to use him more subtly, to comment ironically upon Stoic and Christian maxims. In his soliloquy of IV.iv Antonio's theme is his misfortune (and it is a commonplace of Stoicism that calamities are good for us), but instead of finding consolation in the notion that life is lived on borrowed time (another Stoic commonplace) he derives increased despair from the idea. Next, he cries, 'I'll not blaspheme' (l. 11), but at once proceeds to do so, by prostrating himself in hopeless woe and, wallowing in bleak self-pity, he cries, with heavy irony, 'Behold the valiant'st creature that doth breathe!' (l. 17). Then he defies the ideal of Stoic fortitude by swearing to live, not in order to rise above calamity, but for revenge (also a blasphemous resolution). He concludes by implying a comparison between his situation and Christ on the road to Calvary (l. 23), which has already been suggested by his assumption that he is the epitome of all suffering (l. 16). This web of commentary on the viability or otherwise of the Christian and Stoic creeds is, at first sight, confusing but a larger pattern emerges which effects a compromise between contemplation and action.[67]

According to P. J. Finkelpearl, however, the focus of the play is an attempt to define 'common sense', which, for Marston, is

> the ability to respond with passion to suffering (one's own or another's) and an awareness of man's lot as fundamentally tragic.[68]

He sees in Antonio a demonstration of this quality, while Pandulpho, with his Stoicism, represents one extreme of divergence from it and Balurdo, with his muddled senses, stands for the other.

Balurdo is part 'fool' and part 'foolish courtier'; his habit of noting new words and later using them affectedly is a satire on the gallants who came to the theatre for the sole purpose of garnishing their vocabularies (I.iii.22 n.). As a verbal clown he is not very impressive, although he is a capable 'punning fool' (I.iii.16–21) and his confused synaesthesia is amusing (III.iv.25); but his real talent is musical—he is an accomplished solo voice and himself plays the viol. Marston allows Balurdo a conscience, for he abandons his master Piero, through revulsion at his excesses, and throws in his lot with the conspirators. Through Balurdo's insistance on his due title (I.iii) Marston perhaps intends us to relate him to Sir John Falstaff, recently deceased in *Henry The Fifth* (1599). Occasionally Balurdo's speeches parody the sensationalism of those of Antonio, as when he recounts a comic allegorical dream (I.iii.61–71) immediately after Antonio has described his own dream-vision of his father's ghost (I.iii.39–50). The effect is to relieve the Senecan horror of the main action and to display the witlessness of Balurdo.

Balurdo's simple wits are thematically contrasted with the distraction of Antonio, which is both assumed (IV.i) and, like Hamlet's, sufficiently real to convince his mother (III.ii). Antonio adopts a 'fool's habit' as a disguise at Piero's court (IV.i) and spars verbally with the real fool, Balurdo. The purpose of the scene (iv.ii) is presumably to point to the dramatic irony that Piero, who prefers 'fools' (like the naive villain Strotzo), is undone by one in 'fool's' guise.

Strotzo is another kind of 'fool', simple-minded enough to trust Piero's promises. Strotzo is not without talent, for he is a capable actor, playing the roles assigned him by Piero (as in iii.iii)—but he is a mere foil to his master. His inferiority reveals itself immediately, in his first scene with Piero (i.i), by his inability to complete a statement. Among other male characters Forobosco seeks to moderate the impulsiveness of Piero, and Alberto and Lucio try to perform the same function for Antonio, but it is the Ghost of Andrugio who makes the strongest impression. As a ghost, Andrugio, unlike Hamlet's father, is definite and explicit; because he makes the situation so clear, and because everyone in the play accepts his assessment, he denies both suspense and uncertainty to the plot. One might have hoped for a less dogmatic apparition and one less sure of the moral desirability of revenge (v.v).

Maria is a matron full of humility and tearful pessimism. Her speeches are laden with gnomic remarks, and she is conscious of the historical lesson that her suffering, coupled with Pandulpho's and Antonio's, offers to future ages. In the penultimate scene of the play we catch a glimpse in Maria of Shakespeare's Margaret, widow of Henry VI. Her nurse, Nutriche, is a sib of Juliet's, with the same pragmatic common sense; her consciousness is a scattered confusion between dream and waking. Mellida, daughter to Piero, is a virginal figure of chastity and devotion, who prefers death to dishonour. Against calumny she stands upon her innocence and dies, fittingly, of a broken heart.

In terms of Marston's dramatic development, most of the characters in *Antonio's Revenge* are forward-looking rather than fulfilled. He is hesitant in his portrayal of women, but surer of himself with his masculine villains and philosophers. The dramatic technique of the play as a whole is, however, more mature than the characterisation.

5. THE PLAY IN ITS THEATRE:
'ANTONIO'S REVENGE' AS A SEQUEL

Antonio's Revenge was performed in Paul's playhouse, which appears to have been located in the north-west quadrant of the Chapter House precinct (see frontispiece):[69] as Richard Flecknoe reported, 'on Week-dayes after Vespers . . . the Children of . . . St. Paul's Acted Plays . . . behinde the Convocation-howse in Paul's.[70] The playhouse building was probably originally constructed as a private dwelling house and was being used for this purpose by Reignold Chunnel, one of the bellringers, and his family immediately prior to the revival of plays there in late 1599.[71] While small, with only about 440 square feet on the ground floor available as an auditorium, the building extended into and across the cloisters and was at least two-storeyed; thus it had a sizeable backstage area of about the same square footage as the auditorium.[72] The stage itself may have been built diagonally between the first two main pillars of the cloister in the north-west corner.

Inside, the playhouse had at least two access doors to the main stage (v.i.o.3, 9); adjacent to, or in, one of them was a grating used as a cell window (II.iii.73 and 122.2). These doors flanked a wider door which was curtained and could be left open for use as a discovery space (v.vi.36.1): it may have been wide enough to have allowed processions to enter two abreast (e.g. the dumb show before Act II appears to assume this form of entry). There was a trap (probably in the middle of the stage) large enough to be used as a grave (IV.v.64.1), from which entries could be made (v.ii). The stage appears to have been high enough from the ground to allow easy access beneath it (III.ii.75), and while it was too small to allow spectators to sit on it (*What You Will*, Induction) it could accommodate seventeen actors and a coffin at the same time (II.i.o.2–7), provided the costumes were not too cumbersome.

There was an 'above' (III.ii.75)—and, therefore, space available for a spectators' gallery—which seems to have extended the full width of the main stage; it was a gallery with a dual function, to accommodate the musicians for the entr'acte entertainment and to provide an upper acting area. In conjunction with the main stage, the design of the 'above' created the effect of three house locations; at either side of a central curtained space (I.iii.129.1) there was a *'music house'* (V.v.17.3) and in at least one of these houses (and probably in both) there was an operating casement window (I.iii.130).[73] Paul's stage looked like a street. Marston may have been personally involved in the formulation of this interior design (*cf. Poet.*, III.i.30–5).[74]

In the last two scenes of the play all these acting areas are brought into use. On the main stage the conspirators dance a measure (V.v.17.1); during it, Andrugio's ghost is positioned behind the curtain of the upper acting area (which seems to have been directly above the main discovery space). Piero then calls for a table of sweetmeats (V.v.19) which was set inside the main discovery space, but with the curtain left open. The visual effect is to create a tableau of vengeance; the ghost, who has summoned the avenger, looks down from heaven as 'spectator of revenge' (V.v.22) upon his victim, who is about to consume his own kin and die, his tongue plucked out, unable to cry for mercy or forgiveness. While this execution is in progress the musicians (who flank the ghost in the music houses) and additional choristers (whose voices seem to have been used to supplement the main soloists in the course of the performance) probably provided a funereal accompaniment. The scenes conclude with the drawing of the upper and lower curtains to effect the removal of the ghost of Andrugio (V.v.82.1) and the dead Piero along with the table of sweetmeats (V.vi.36.1).

No elaborate properties were needed for the performance of *Antonio's Revenge* (although, in case of need, the Paul's Boys seem to have been in the habit of hiring special effects, probably from the Globe).[75] A bleeding human body (I.iii.129.1), assorted severed human limbs (V.v.49.1), a tomb (III.1.0.7), a coffin (II.i.0.4), a bass viol (III.iv.16.1), a child's bubble-pipe (IV.i.0.1–2), and a variety of weapons—all these are common properties for the Elizabethan stage.

The theatre, situated in the Chapter House precinct, was conveniently located close to a main London thoroughfare, the north-south aisle of Paul's. Not even during divine service was there any cessation in the traffic of 'Porters, Butchers watercbcarcrs . . .

[who] . . . Carrye and recarrie whatever, no man wth standinge them or gaynsayinge the[m] w[ch] is a greate scandall to honest mynded men, and boies . . . pissinge upon stones, by St. ffaithes dore, to slide upon as uppon ysse'.[76] The paving of this thoroughfare was broken and the church was 'verie noysomlie kepte by reason of Certaine heaps of durte and other filthie thynge in many Corners'.[77] Passers-by could buy beer, ale and tobacco from the Minor Canons' Buttery; it was common to drink, gamble and smoke during services;[78] one could go up into the steeple and disturb the congregation by throwing stones or 'whooping' and 'hallowing'.[79] Apart from a multitude of beggars and 'woemen wth Children in their Armes and other poore folkes almost always sittinge aboute the pillers of the Church',[80] the north–south aisle was a place of business where lawyers met clients and masters met servants, where one could consult, among others, bookbinders, schoolteachers, joiners, carpenters, glaziers, stationers, mercers, hosiers, trunk-makers, all of whom had shops in the church. A boy publicising a play at the adjacent theatre by crying the title aloud in the main aisle would be assured of a ready audience.[81]

From 1584 the master of the children was Thomas Gyles, but in April 1599 he was too ill to give a report on the choir to Bishop Bancroft[82] and he was superseded by Edward Pearce, whose appointment dates from 11 May in that year.[83] Gyles was dead in July 1600.[84] He had been a conscientious master, however, and the choir under his direction were acknowledged to be skilled in music and fit for their places.[85] When Pearce was appointed, Marston seems to have become almost immediately involved with the Paul's Boys, possibly through an acquaintance with Ambrose Goulding, the Senior Cardinal, who was responsible for the Christian education of the choristers and who was priest in charge at St Gregory's by Paul's and held a curacy in Sergeants Inn.[86]

Officially there were ten choristers (although *Antonio's Revenge* needs at least seventeen actors) maintained, at no expense to the promotors of their plays, by an income of £50 per annum from the Dean and Chapter and £20 per annum from the rent of certain almonry houses.[87] They were skilled in music[88] (the play has seven songs) and were professionally expert in masque (as for the masque-of-avengers). The Duke of Stettin–Pomerania, an early seventeenth-century tourist, is full of praise for the quality of the music produced by the 'Children's Comoediam',

> For a whole hour before [the beginning of the play] a delightful performance of musicam instrumentalem is given on organs, lutes, pandores, mandolines, violins, and flutes; and a boy's singing cum voce tremula . . . so tunefully, that we have not heard the like of it on the whole journey, except perhaps the nuns of Milan did it better.[89]

The attraction of the child actors, who would be fully trained in the elaborate language of rhetorical gesture,[90] was not in itself of a whimsical or even perverse quality. The medieval tradition, the most formative influence on the Elizabethan consciousness, possessed little awareness of the sequential development from infancy to adulthood; a child was a non-participant in human affairs until the age of ten, and then, without gradual transition, became an adult-in-miniature.[91] These diminutive adults were full members of society, limited naturally in terms of physical capacity but capable of contracting alliances, fighting, commanding. As actors they had definite advantages over men. The physical similarity of a beardless youth and a young girl turned the romance convention of the friendship of two young men or two girls, when one was a disguised member of the other sex, from an improbability into a plausibility; their youth and inexperience could be utilised for delicate dramatic effect, suggesting the irony implicit in the reflection of adult characteristics; their full participation in the real world allowed the portrayal of tyrant or lover, without any necessary suggestion of incongruity.[92] Although the choirboys were trained in the formal language of rhetoric, this does not necessarily mean that their acting was stylised: they were skilled in the use of face, voice, gesture and attitude to convey feeling, which would help to compensate for their lack of experience.

It is likely that *Antonio and Mellida* was the first play performed by the newly revived Paul's company before an audience of less than one hundred spectators, who may have voluntarily rewarded the actors for the entertainment provided and who found themselves in close proximity with the stage and the performers, because the playhouse building was very small.[93] At the close of the Induction a sequel is promised, provided that the play is well received: this sequel is *Antonio's Revenge*. While there is a radical change of theme from the 'comic crosses of true love' in *Antonio and Mellida* (v.ii.264) to the horrors of *Antonio's Revenge*, where 'Never more woe in lesser plot was found' (v.vi.59), the narrative of the tyranny of Piero begun in the former play is completed in the latter. In addition there is a considerable degree of continuity between the two plays in terms of their purpose and their mode of presentation.

The Induction and Prologue to *Antonio and Mellida* disclaim any serious dramatic or intellectual intention and insist that the purpose is solely to please the particular select group of spectators who have assembled at the theatre. In the same way, the Prologue to *Antonio's Revenge* deliberately subordinates the play to a fashionable congruity between the winter season and the tragic drama offered. This attitude—that taste is more important than dramatic context—is a fashionable pose maintained throughout both plays.

The two plays contain a number of similarities of incident and character: Balurdo reminds us in *Antonio's Revenge* (III.iv.49–50) that he was knighted for winning a singing contest (*I Ant. & Mel.*, v.ii.28); Antonio falls prostrate twice to lament his woes (*I Ant. & Mel.*, II.i.200 and IV.i.164.1) and repeats the action in *Antonio's Revenge*, IV.iv.11.1); the situation in *Antonio and Mellida* where Antonio's death is reported to Mellida while he, disguised as an Amazon, looks on (II.i.152 ff) is repeated in *Antonio's Revenge*, with Antonio this time disguised as a fool (IV.iii.74 ff). *Antonio and Mellida* offers eight songs; *Antonio's Revenge* seven: both plays have masques (*I Ant. & Mel.*, v.ii.69.1–21; *Ant. Rev.*, v.v.0.2.) and both deliberately exploit verbal ingenuity as an attraction. By the end of their respective first acts both plays have introduced a new word to the audience on the average every fifteen lines. Similarly both plays make maximum use of the scenic possibilities afforded by the facilities of the Paul's stage and deliberately draw attention to this exploitation.[94]

Antonio and Mellida and *Antonio's Revenge* both make extensive use of mime to act as commentary upon the main spoken action: Marston develops the traditional dumb show to make theatrically innovative statements.[95] This can be seen in the first act of *Antonio and Mellida*, where, after Mellida has been told of the drowning of Antonio, she is taken out to dance by her rejected suitors; Piero's approval of these suitors and her antagonism is reflected by this enforced gaiety: a form of visual dramatic irony. Similarly in *Antonio's Revenge*, the show before Act II, although a conventional funeral procession, is staged in order to reveal to the audience the name of the murderer while leaving the actors ignorant of the assassin's identity—again a form of visual dramatic irony. Piero's opening speech to this act, 'Rot there, thou cerecloth' (II.i.1), is a satirical comment upon the preceding show: Marston is deliberately playing off a rhetorical against a visual effect.

Throughout *Antonio's Revenge* Marston assumes that his audience is familiar with contemporary theatre, particularly with the plays of Shakespeare. At the conclusion of the first scene of the first act, Piero consciously imitates Richard of Gloucester's claims (*R3*, I.ii.230) with his boast 'Poison the father, butcher the son, and marry the mother' (104), and Act III opens like the scene in the tomb of the Capulets of *Romeo and Juliet* (v.iii). Similarly the dumb show before Act III, which is the most complex visual effect attempted in the play, is preoccupied with Piero's wooing of Maria seen in terms of Richard's wooing of Anne in *Richard III*. Piero's approach to Maria, especially when he '*tears open his breast*' (III.i.0.9) invites the spectator to compare it with Shakespeare's wooing scene. In the act which follows it is assumed, on the analogy of Anne's acceptance of Richard, that Maria has accepted Piero. The show before the fifth act reveals the web of revenge, presided over by the Ghost of Andrugio, drawing together about Piero, but he remains unaware of it—another instance of visual dramatic irony. The act then opens with a speech by the Ghost of Andrugio which emerges naturally from the preceding show; Marston has here organically related a mime, and the rhetorical commentary which stems from it, to the unfolding of the plot.

Marston's use of the dumb show is a sophistication of the old theatrical custom of introducing acts by visual warnings of special climaxes. In the first two shows it is Piero who is dominant and triumphant; he is resisted passively but his schemes are apparently successful. The turning-point of the action is indicated by the third show before the fifth act, which occurs immediately after the philosophical crisis of the play in the last scene of the fourth act. This dumb show, which emphasises the unanimity of the opposition to Piero—even Maria draws a knife—foreshadows the coming triumph of Vengeance and Piero's consequent overthrow.

Concurrent with this 'dumb action' is a complex pattern of musical statement which also acts as a running commentary on tyranny and revenge. In the first movement of the play, after the waking of the bridegroom by music (I.ii.61.1), the gentle aubade of Antonio beneath the bride's, Mellida's, window contrasts ironically with the stark surprise of the 'discovery' of the bloody remains of Feliche (I.iii.129.1–2). The last thirty-eight lines of the final scene of the act, during which Pandulpho advocates a policy of Stoic *apathia*, are spoken to a background musical accompaniment—perhaps performed as a type of recitative—and the act concludes with a call for 'louder music' with a 'sad tone', a dirge to suit the dismal situation.

In the second act,

> Piero is marked by a deliberately perverse use of music. As he gloatingly watches Antonio speaking with Mellida at the prison grating he turns to Strotzo, saying[96]
>> He grieves; laugh, Strotzo, laugh; he weeps.
>> . . . Strotzo, cause me straight
>> Some plaining ditty to augment despair.
>> [II.iii.125, 128–9]

In the third act the comical music of the songs of Balurdo (III.iv) is used as an ironic lyric interlude before the second shock discovery of the play, the ghost of Andrugio revealed behind the curtains of Maria's bed (III.iv.63.1–2). In the fourth act Piero demands stately music to solemnise his exit (IV.iii.198), but the conspirators against him reject music in a manner reminiscent of *Antonio and Mellida*. In the former play Marston directs (IV.i.155.1) '*The boy runs a note*: ANTONIO *breaks it*'—the sudden rupturing of a held tone, to emphasise Mellida's grief. In *Antonio's Revenge* when Antonio,

Alberto and Pandulpho are about the burial of Feliche and
Antonio asks the Page

> Will't sing a dirge, boy ?   [IV.v.65]

Pandulpho and Alberto deliberately misunderstand him and
assume that he is alluding ironically to the dead Feliche,

> *Pan.* No; no song; 'twill be vile out of tune.
> *Alb.* Indeed he's hoarse; the poor boy's voice is cracked.
>   [IV.v.66–7]

While Piero may continue to use music for merely ceremonial
purposes, the effects of his tyranny are to cause the breakdown of
the musical ability both microcosmically in Feliche and macro-
cosmically, for 'All the strings of nature's symphony/Are cracked
and jar' (IV.v.69–70). In the last act Piero's self-infatuation is
emphasised when he calls,

> Mount a lofty note,
> Fill red-cheeked Bacchus, let Lyaeus float
> In burnished goblets!   [V.iv.19–21]

Like Hamlet's Claudius, he drinks to music and then anticipates
with relish the 'light lavoltas' (V.iv.22) for his wedding, but these
quickly metamorphose themselves into the menacing ballet of the
avengers. The play concludes with another dialogue to music,
during and probably after which the choir sang a cantata based on
the phrase 'Mellida is dead'.

This carefully articulated pattern of mime and music is con-
trolled within a framework that is classical in its formal purity.
Time in the play is strictly limited to two days, and

> the use of striking clocks, entries with torches or tapers, and
> frequent references to dawn, day-break, nightfall, sunshine and
> moonlight, mark the passing of the hours.[97]

Act I begins at 2 a.m., with Piero having murdered Andrugio and
Feliche since midnight: Maria arrives at 5 a.m. (I.ii.29) and
Antonio wakes with 'infant morn' (I.iii.1). Act II occupies the
daylight of this first day, and extends into the evening from
the rising of the moon (II.iii.76) until midnight, at which time the
third act begins. The whole of this act takes place during the

second night (*cf.* III.ii.93) and it concludes with earliest dawn (III.v.33). The fourth act occupies the ensuing daylight, and the vengeance of the last act is consummated during the torchlight of the third night-time; it ends before dawn has broken (v.vi.7). Marston has deliberately telescoped his action into a period of some forty-eight hours to emphasise the immediacy and anguish of the conflicts between the principals. He exploits the contrasts between light and darkness: each act, except the fourth, begins with a scene in torchlight; the fourth has all its scenes in daylight, but it both follows and precedes acts in which all the scenes are artificially lit. So obvious is this use of light and shade that Marston may have been experimenting with lighting effects, at least to the extent of requiring the 'tireman' to light and extinguish candles to set the mood for different acts.[98]

Despite the obvious technical virtuosity of these staging arrangements and the care with which they are integrated into the structure of the play as a whole, no unanimity of opinion exists as to what Marston's overall dramatic purpose was. The most influential modern view is that of R. A. Foakes, who believes that *Antonio and Mellida* and *Antonio's Revenge* are a parody of earlier revenge plays. They

> work from the beginning as vehicles for child actors consciously ranting in oversize parts, and we are not allowed to take their passions or motives seriously. Their grand speeches are undermined by bathos or parody, and spring from no developed situation, so that we are not moved by them, and do not take them seriously enough to demand justice at the end.[99]

This is an attractive argument, for it turns Marston's dramatic vices of overstatement into the exaggerating virtues of the satirist. But to assume that burlesque of the revenge tradition is Marston's motivating intention in *Antonio's Revenge* is an oversimplification of a much more complex situation.

In his music-accompanied dialogue at the end of the first act Pandulpho advocates and has himself adopted a passivity in the face of tyranny and grief which is an amalgam of Christian humility and Stoic passionlessness. He refuses to resort to the grossness of histrionics,

> Wouldst have me turn rank mad,
> Or wring my face with mimic action,
> Stamp, curse, weep, rage, and then my bosom strike?
> Away, 'tis apish action, player-like.   [77–80]

He finds sufficient emotional support in his grief for the loss of his son in his own resolute mind (l. 99). Early in the second act, tempted to action when Piero condemns Mellida and tyrannously refuses to allow Feliche to be buried, Pandulpho restrains himself and contemptuously rejects Piero's threats by putting forward the ultimate Stoic-personal mode of triumph over the world, suicide (II.ii.85–8). In the next scene Antonio, in contrast to this acceptance of passivity in the face of tyranny and grief, can find no consolation in Stoicism—he rejects Seneca on the grounds that his philosophy bears no substantial relation to the actualities of suffering (II.iii.49 ff.): he sees the need for some form of action (106 ff.). Aided by the ghost of Andrugio, he resolves upon vengeance, and he finds philosophical support, ironically, again in Seneca but this time from the tragedies (III.ii.15 ff.); he acts unrestrainedly in executing Julio (III.iii) and can then outface the ghost (III.v), subsequently justifying his action on the Machiavellian grounds of expediency (IV.i.20 ff.) with himself acting as supreme arbiter of right and wrong (IV.i.30–3). This antithesis between Pandulpho's and Antonio's conclusions and behaviour is maintained consistently as a contrast between the conduct of a boy and that of an adult: for Pandulpho, from the outset, is treated as a man (I.v.68 ff.), whereas Antonio is spoken of as a 'sweet youth' (I.v.70) and behaves often like a child. Thus Antonio enters in Act IV with a child's *'little toy of a walnut shell and soap to make bubbles'* and then proceeds to prostrate himself in hopeless grief at the loss of Mellida, lamenting, 'I am a poor, poor orphan; a weak, weak child' (IV.iv.14).

A change is dramatised, however, in the last scene of the fourth act, where the philosophical crisis of the play is reached, concurrently with the climax of a maturing process for the boys who act the parts. Now Pandulpho's passivity gives way, under the compulsion of events, to an argument for action against Piero. At the same time he realises that while he had assumed himself to be mature (as others had also done) he had, through his total rejection of action for contemplation, been behaving like a child (IV.v.47 ff.). He joins the conspirators together in a united effort to overthrow Piero, and from this point onwards all childishness and childlike characteristics vanish from the play. The three principal conspirators are united in the maturing of their purpose, for Pandulpho, until then passive, and Antonio, until then unrestrained and reckless, combine in deliberated action. This scene also represents the moment of the metamorphosis of these choirboy actors into men, made mature by the pressure of Piero's tyranny.

In the penultimate scene of the play the dramatic form is concluded with the fulfilment of the vengeance, but in the philosophical and operatic sense it remains incomplete. There has, as yet, been no musical counterpart to the quasi-operatic philosophical statement at the end of Act I. The musical close is provided by the concluding cantata in honour of Mellida, and the philosophical completion by a return to the opening thematic movement. At the end of the first act Pandulpho advocated a life of Christian and Stoic humility, but this view is now modified by tyranny-induced anguish, and matured and married to a commitment to action. As the play ends the conspirators avow to

> live enclosed
> In holy verge of some religious order,
> Most constant votaries.   [v.vi.34–6]

The life of prayer is undertaken as a penance for the action which forced these erstwhile Stoics to become assassins. Tyranny must be overthrown, even at the cost of child murder, but the ensuing debt to the 'dread power' (v.vi.33) is lifelong.

Coupled with this evaluative attitude towards the philosophical arguments for and against action is an advocacy of a certain self-retirement, a studied casualness of manner, a deliberate refusal to indulge in the expression of intense emotion. This is the impassivity with which Pandulpho can face the worst that fate can do, an attitude which Antonio attempts to imitate but is able only to parody, as when he abandons Mellida to her fate in prison, crying absurdly

> Behold a prostrate wretch laid on his tomb;
> His epitaph thus: *Ne plus ultra*. Ho!
> Let none out-woe me, mine's Herculean woe.
>
> [II.iii.131–3]

Antonio's concern with himself, boasting about his own import-
ance as a sufferer, appears to us to outweigh the significance of why
he is suffering and for whom. Marston, however, seems anxious
that his audience should acknowledge the viability of such an
ironic stance, in its correctly balanced form; he dedicates *Antonio
and Mellida* to 'the most honourably renowned Nobody' and
consistently breaks dramatic illusion to create an intimate sense of
shared decorum with the spectators. His characters share private
jokes with their audience—like Balurdo appearing with a beard
which will not stick on and making exasperated remarks about the
inefficiency of the tireman (II.i.21 and n.). Since beards were not
used at Paul's,[100] this represents a deliberately startling breach of
dramatic illusion and theatrical practice which serves to draw the
audience closer to the context of the play. Later when Pandulpho
explains his Stoical reticence and declares

> Why, all this while I ha' but played a part,
> Like to some boy that acts a tragedy,
> Speaks burly words and raves out passion;
> But when he thinks upon his infant weakness,
> He droops his eye.   [IV.v.47–51]

Marston seems to be suggesting that a boy actor, conscious of his
limitations, is able to project the realities of grief because he is
aware that he is taking part in a mimetic act. It is this frank acceptance of inadequacy that saves the boy actor from pretentiousness,
and intensifies the feelings portrayed, by the implication that
mimesis itself breaks down in the attempt to convey adequately
the agonies of the human dilemma.

Many critics, however, have felt that the ending of the play is
morally ambiguous, since Antonio does not overtly express guilt
or suffer punishment for the murder of Julio.[101] It is indeed true
that, seen purely in terms of its revenge tragedy structure, the play
presents Antonio as blameless, and seems to acknowledge that he

acted as a dutiful son should, in the appeasement of his father's ghost by shedding the blood of the murderer and his kindred. But such an explanation of the revenge—that the play wholly commends Antonio's action and the modern reader wholly abhors it—ignores the coincidence in the plot of a pseudo-operatic and philosophical form with a purely dramatic structure. Marston is seeking to make a complex, and it must be admitted not always explicit, statement through the medium of conventional revenge tragedy combined with and qualified by the very unconventional mime and music of the choristers, producing a hybrid that has obvious affinities with opera. The act of lifelong contrition, retiring from the very activity in life to which he had committed himself, will be Antonio's penance. His liturgical, almost monastic, statement is solemnised by the closing requiem for the departed sung by the choristers in a specifically ecclesiastical setting.

If the play had no sixth scene in the final act, Antonio would remain a sanguinary villain-hero who forfeits any understanding or sympathy from the spectator. But the concluding scene shifts this focus and ends the play operatically with the suggestion that in terms of macro-cosmic understanding the music from heaven provides the final comprehension. The characters, who are also choirboys, have matured in the course of playing their roles, thus overcoming their feelings of inadequacy as expressed in the Induction to *Antonio and Mellida*, so that now they can offer a meaningful fusion of music and drama. It is in this development of a quasi-operatic performance that *Antonio's Revenge* represented for its age a significant and efficient rival to the dramatically incomparably superior *Hamlet*.

6. STAGE HISTORY

The sensation caused by Jonson's attack on Marston and Dekker in *Poetaster*, and Dekker's ripost in *Satiromastix*, was brief. After their initial enthusiasm the playgoing public reacted unfavourably. In *Wittes Pilgrimage* (1605) John Davies of Hereford explains that the 'war of the poets' led to a loss of custom by the boys and, presumably, to a decline in popularity of plays like *Antonio's Revenge*:

That Poets should be made to vomit words,
[As being so rawe Wittes Mawe could not digest]
Hath to Wittes praise, bin as so many swords,
To kill it quite in earnest, and in Iest,
Then, to untrusse him [before Knights, and Lords]
Whose Muse hath power, to untrusse what nott ?
Was a vaine cast, though cast to hitt a Blott.
O Imps of Phoebus, whie, ô why doe yee
Imploy the Pow'r of your Divinity
(Which should but foyle vice from which we should flee!)
Upon impeaching your owne Quality ?[102]

The final development of the dispute was a vulgarisation; the boys
forfeited much of their effectiveness as satirists by indulging in a
public brawl. A similar awareness is present in the mind of
Shakespeare when Hamlet remarks to Rosencrantz of the boy
players,

> will they not say afterwards if they should grow themselves to
> common players (as it is like most will if their means are not
> better) their writers do them wrong, to make them exclaim against
> their own succession ?   [II.ii.350–4]

The Poetomachia in its character as a boy–adult controversy was
liable to deny the boys their potential future careers as adult
professionals.[103]

As far as the annals of theatrical history are concerned, Jonson's
parody seems to have assassinated *Antonio's Revenge*.[104] Even
without *Poetaster*, however, the theme of Marston's play was overshadowed for the seventeenth and subsequent centuries by Shakespeare's *Hamlet*. That Jonson did not like it is no good reason for
not producing it. *Antonio's Revenge* was created as an experimental
production for a 'little theatre'; it remains capable of being
produced in a number of ways (particularly as a parody of *Hamlet*).
The time for its revival is long overdue.

7. SYNOPSIS OF PART I OF 'ANTONIO AND MELLIDA'

Piero Sforza, Duke of Venice, has defeated the Genoese fleet under
the command of Andrugio, Duke of Genoa, and his son, Antonio.
To further his dynastic ambitions Piero plans to match his

daughter, Mellida, with an Italian suitor other than Antonio, with whom she is in love. Antonio and Andrugio, however, are separately cast ashore on Venetian territory. Antonio makes his way to Piero's court, disguised as an Amazon, and persuades Mellida to flee with him. In their flight they meet Andrugio, but Mellida is captured and returned to her father's court. Andrugio proceeds to court with the coffin of his son and claims the reward offered by Piero,

> We vow by the honor of our birth to recompense any man that bringeth Andrugio's head with twenty thousand double pistolets and the endearing to our choicest love. [v.ii.137–9]

Ostensibly overcome by this act of valour, Piero wishes Antonio resurrected, at which point Antonio arises from the coffin; Piero is reconciled to Andrugio and accepts Antonio as his son-in-law; a general rejoicing is proclaimed.

NOTES

1 W. W. Greg, *A Bibliography of the English Printed Drama to the Restoration* (1939), I, 17.
2 *Ibid.*, I, 185.
3 *Ibid.*
4 *Antonio and Mellida and Antonio's Revenge*, ed. W. W. Greg (*M.S.R.*, 1921), pp. x–xi.
5 H. N. Hillebrand, *The Child Actors* (Urbana, Ill., 1926), p. 111.
6 Greg, *Bibliography*, III, 1089–90. Sheares's Preface to the 1633 edition, first issue, appears in Appendix A.
7 'Bibliographical notes on some Marston Quartos and early collected editions', *Libr.* VIII (1928), 344–5.
8 Thomas Fisher entered the *Antonio* plays with Mathew Lownes on 24 October 1601, after which nothing is known of him. In 1633 *Antonio's Revenge* was derelict, as was *What You Will*, owned by T. Thorp (entry of 6 August 1607), for Thorp appears to go into a decline after *c.* 1609; his last entry (3 November 1624) is a transfer of rights. On the other hand *Antonio and Mellida* was clearly owned by M. Young (entry of 6 December 1630). The case of *Sophonisba* and *The Dutch Courtesan* is rather different, for both appear to have been owned by the widow of J. Hodgettes (*ob. c.* December 1625). On 25 January 1625/6 she assigned four copies (no Marston was included) to R. Allott in consideration of £45. How Sheares escaped litigation from this grasping widow remains a mystery. (Entries from E. Arber, *A Transcript of the Stationers' Register* (1876).)

9 *The Dramatic Records of Sir Henry Herbert*, ed. J. Q. Adams (Cornell, 1917), p. 21.

10 W. W. Greg, in a review of 'E. M. Albright, *Dramatic Publication in England, 1580–1640*, New York, 1927', *R.E.S.*, 4 (1928), 97.

11 There are copies in the libraries of the British Museum, the Bodleian, the Victoria and Albert Museum, the University of Texas, Harvard University, Yale University, Boston Public Library, the Folger Shakespeare Library, the Carl H. Pforzheimer Library, the Henry E. Huntington Library, and one owned by Mr R. H. Taylor of Princeton: to all owners I am indebted for access to their copies.

12 Since this Quarto is well printed and without extant proof corrections, an analysis of the compositors failed (in my judgement) to yield information of value in the reconstruction of the text.

13 The details of Marston's life were largely established by R. E. Brettle in a series of articles, *M.L.R.* 22 (1927), 7–14; 317–19; *R.E.S.* 3 (1927), 398–405; 4 (1928), 212–14; 13 (1962), 390–3; 16 (1965), 396–9. His biography has also been recounted in a number of recent volumes, e.g. A. José Axelrad, *Un Malcontent Elizabéthain, John Marston* (Paris, 1955), *passim*, and A. Davenport (ed.), *The Poems of John Marston* (Liverpool, 1961), pp. 1–6.

14 Marston's father calls himself 'of city of Coventry Gent.' in his will; see M. S. Allen, *The Satire of John Marston* (New York, 1965) p. 5. A. à Wood thought Marston, the dramatist, had been born in Coventry, *Athenae Oxonienses*, ed. P. Bliss (1831), I, 762.

15 A detailed discussion of this affair is provided by A. Davenport (ed.), *The Collected Poems of Joseph Hall* (Liverpool, 1949), pp. xxviii–xxxiv.

16 They were probably related through the Guarsi family; see R. E. Brettle, *R.E.S.*, 16 (1965), 396–9.

17 P. J. Finkelpearl, *H. L. Q.*, 29 (1966), 223–34.

18 *Diary*, ed. W. W. Greg (1904), I, 112.

19 Chambers, *E.S.*, III, 428.

20 P. J. Finkelpearl, *John Marston of the Middle Temple* (Harvard, 1969), p. 84.

21 See 'Stage history'.

22 Jonson, *Works*, ed. J. H. Herford and P. Simpson (Oxford, 1925), I, 140.

23 A detailed analysis of the staging of *I Ant. & Mel.*, *Ant. Rev.*, *J. Drum's Ent.* and *What You Will* will be found in my 'Presentation of plays at Second Paul's: the early phase (1599–1602)', *Elizabethan Theatre VI*, ed. G. R. Hibbard (Toronto, 1977), pp. 21–47.

24 C. Brown (ed.), *Poems by Sir John Salusbury and Robert Chester*, *E.E.T.S.*, Extra Series, 113 (1914), lxxii.

25 Exact dates, or indeed the order of composition, of the two plays *The Dutch Courtesan* and *The Malcontent* are, in our present state of knowledge, impossible to assign: my order is conjectural.

26 *Remaines*, p. 8.

27 Chambers, *E.S.*, III, 254–6: Chambers believes Marston escaped. The offensive remarks in *Eastward Ho!* were made by Seagull: 'you shal live freely there [in America], without Sergeants, or Courtiers,

or Lawyers, or Intelligencers, onely a few industrious Scots perhaps, who indeed are disperst over the face of the whole earth. But as for them, there are no greater friends to Englishmen and *England*, when they are out an't, in the world, then they are. And for my part, I would a hundred thousand of 'hem were there, for wee are all one Countreymen now, yee know; and we shoulde finde ten times more comfort of them there, then wee doe heere' (Wood, III.128).

28 Marston was probably invited to write this entertainment because of his earlier association with William Stanley at Paul's. The letter is first printed in Historical Manuscripts Commission, Manuscripts in Various Collections 7.389.

29 F. P. Wilson, *M.L.R.*, 9 (1914), 99.

30 J. George, *N. & Q.*, 202 (1957), 226.

31 After his ordination Marston's literary career appears to have ceased; unless he is the author of certain satires against Buckingham attributed to him by R. E. Brettle, 'John Marston and the Duke of Buckingham, 1627–28', *N. & Q.*, 212 (1967), 326–30.

32 Jonson, *Works*, I, 138.

33 See p. 4.

34 *Athenae Oxonienses*, I, 763.

35 *M.L.R.*, 22 (1927), 318–19.

36 Chambers, *E.S.*, III, 429–30.

37 D. J. McGinn, 'A new date for *Antonio's Revenge*', *P.M.L.A.*, 53 (1938), 135.

38 N. Coghill, *Shakespeare's Professional Skills* (Cambridge, 1965), p. 14.

39 J. H. Smith, L. D. Pizer and E. K. Kaufman, '*Hamlet*, *Antonio's Revenge* and the *Ur-Hamlet*', *Sh.Q.*, IX (1958), 493–8.

40 *Ibid.*, p. 496.

41 Jonson, *Works*, I, 415.

42 Balurdo's song (IV.iii.153–9) may be an allusion to the ballads on the death of Essex (25 February 1601), for, as the Duke of Stettin–Pomerania recorded (on 16 September 1602), 'How beloved and admired this Earl was throughout the Kingdom, may be judged from the circumstances that his song, in which he takes leave of the Queen and the whole country, is sung and played on musical instruments all over the country' (*Diary*, *Trans. of the Royal Hist. Soc.*, N.S., 6 (1892), 15): see IV.iii.153 n. It remains perfectly possible, however, that the allusion is accidental (the themes were very common) or that the song is an addition to the play at a date later than its performance.

43 W. R. Gair, 'La Compagnie des Enfants de St. Paul (1599–1606)', *Dramaturgie et Société* (Paris, 1968), II, 661, and 'Presentation of plays', *op. cit.*, *passim*.

44 I. Smith, *Shakespeare's Blackfriars Playhouse* (New York, 1964), p. 180.

45 D. L. Frost, a recent advocate of the '*Antonio's Revenge* derives from *Hamlet*' theory, admits that there are no verbal similarities 'sufficiently close to be quoted'. (*The School of Shakespeare*, Cambridge, 1968, p. 181 n.).

46 Preface to Greene's *Menaphon*, in *The Works of Thomas Nashe*, ed. R. B. McKerrow, rev. F. P. Wilson (Oxford, 1958), III, 315.

47 It has been argued that this early Hamlet play was a first version by Shakespeare himself; but conclusive evidence is lacking.

48 All three of these versions of the Hamlet story (together with a translation of Grammaticus' Latin original) may be found in an edition by Sir I. Gollancz, *The Sources of Hamlet* (Oxford, 1967).

49 H. H. Furness (ed.), *The New Variorum Shakespeare, Hamlet* (Philadelphia, Pa., 1918), II, 89. While *Hamblet* is a translation of Belleforest it adds certain details derived, apparently, from Shakespeare's *Hamlet*, e.g. when killing the eavesdropping councillor Hamlet cries, 'A rat, a rat!' (*Sources of Hamlet*, p. 207), a detail not in Belleforest but found in *Hamlet*, III.iv.22.

50 F. S. Boas, *The Works of Thomas Kyd* (Oxford, 1926), p. xlvi.

51 *Sources of Hamlet*, p. 101.

52 Frost, *op. cit.*, pp. 175–6.

53 Hunter was the first editor to identify the allusions to Whyttynton.

54 (1901), p. 62 n.

55 *The Age of Shakespeare* (1908), p. 115.

56 'John Marston', *The Criterion*, 13 (1933–34), 583, 584.

57 *The Jacobean Drama* (1953), p. 83.

58 These statistics are purely tentative; a revision of *O.E.D.* could bring about substantial antedating.

59 *Seneca and Elizabethan Tragedy* (Cambridge, 1922), p. 125.

60 A. H. Thorndike, 'The relation of *Hamlet* to contemporary revenge plays', *P.M.L.A.*, 2 (1902), 125.

61 *Elizabethan Revenge Tragedy, 1587–1642* (Gloucester, Mass., 1959), p. 120.

62 *John Marston of the Middle Temple* (Harvard, 1969), p. 150.

63 *The Enchanted Glass* (Oxford, 1950), p. 177.

64 *Elizabethan Revenge Tragedy*, p. 122.

65 *Jacobean Drama*, p. 88 n.

66 'Stoicism and revenge in Marston', *E.S.*, 51 (1970), 512.

67 See below, 'The play in its theatre'.

68 *John Marston of the Middle Temple*, p. 151.

69 See 'Presentation of plays', pp. 39–47.

70 Chambers, *E.S.*, IV, 364.

71 *The Visitation Book of Bishop Bancroft*, 1598; Guildhall MS 9537/9 f. 47v.

72 A detailed analysis of the interior of the Paul's playhouse will be found in 'Presentation of plays', *op. cit.*, pp. 36–7.

73 *Ibid.*, p. 37.

74 *Ibid.*, p. 36.

75 *Ibid.*, p. 38.

76 *Visitation Book*, f. 45.

77 *Ibid.*, f. 46v.

78 *Ibid.*, f. 61.

79 *Ibid.*, ff. 44v, 46v.

80 *Ibid.*, f. 52v.

81 *Cf. Northward Ho !*, IV.i.251.

82 *Visitation Book*, f. 18.

83 St Paul's Cathedral; *Dean and Chapter Registers, Nowell* III, f. 154.

84 St Gregory by Paul's, *Register*, 4 July 1600.

85 *Visitation Book*, f. 47v.

86 See 'Presentation of plays', pp. 21–2.

87 *Visitation Book*, f. 47v.

88 *Ibid.*

89 *Diary*, 28 September 1602.

90 See B. L. Joseph, *Elizabethan Acting* (Oxford, 1964), *passim*.

91 Balurdo and Flavia (of *I Ant. & Mel.*) appear to have been about
    fourteen, but others in the cast were smaller and younger (see
    'Presentation of plays', p. 26). While two of the Paul's boys were
    members of the choir in 1594 and in 1598, the entire company had
    changed by 1607, but in that year one of the boys was twelve (if he is
    the same Henry Burnett who was baptised in the adjacent parish of
    St Martin Ludgate on 6 April 1595). There is some suggestion that
    the composition of the choir partially altered between *I Ant. & Mel.*
    and *Ant. Rev.*, because Feliche appears only as a corpse in the latter
    play and Alberto speaks of his voice as having 'cracked' (IV.v.67). This
    may imply that when they were no longer suitable as choristers, Paul's
    retained experienced boys as actors. The age range, then, extended
    from less than twelve to puberty and beyond. Perhaps some of the
    older actors at Paul's were in their mid-teens. (Hillebrand, pp. 111–12,
    prints the lists of choristers.)

92 See P. Ariès, *Centuries of Childhood*, trans. R. Baldick (1926), *passim*.

93 This analysis and the following interpretation of *Ant. Rev.* are
    substantially based on factual evidence presented in 'Presentation of
    plays', *op. cit.*

94 By the end of the first act of *I Ant. & Mel.* all the acting areas have
    been used and the entire company presented to the audience; see
    'Presentation of plays', pp. 23–4.

95 I am indebted to Dieter Mehl's *The Elizabethan Dumb Show* (1968),
    pp. 125–34, for some aspects of this analysis of Marston's use of mime.

96 R. W. Ingram, 'The use of music in the plays of John Marston',
    Music and Letters, 39 (1956), 160.

97 J. W. Lever, *The Tragedy of State* (1971), p. 25.

98 See 'Presentation of plays', pp. 30, 38.

99 'John Marston's fantastical plays: *Antonio and Mellida* and *Antonio's
    Revenge*', *P.Q.*, 41 (1962), 236.

100 See William Percy, *Arabia Sitiens* (Alnwick Castle MS 509), 'Here he
    held him by the Bearde, or clawd him on the face. If for Poules this,
    Bearde for th'other'. Percy's plays were written for performance at
    Paul's—see 'Presentation of plays', p. 27.

101 See, for example, F. Bowers, *Elizabethan Revenge Tragedy, 1587–
    1642* (Gloucester, Mass., 1959), p. 124, and C. V. Boyer, *The Villain
    as Hero in Elizabethan Tragedy* (1914), p. 134.

102 *The Complete Poems of John Davies*, ed. A. B. Grosart (Edinburgh,
    1878), II, 37.

103 There are several studies of the Poetomachia, but most of them highly conjectural, e.g. J. H. Penniman, *The War of the Theatres* (Philadelphia, Pa., 1897); R. A. Small, *The Stage Quarrel between Ben Jonson and the So-called Poetasters* (Breslau, 1899). R. B. Sharpe, *The Real War of the Theatres* (Baltimore, Md., 1935) sees the issues purely in terms of the rivalry between the theatres. My views on the controversy are based on my own analysis, cited at n. 43.

104 There is one exception. Professor J. E. Kramer (Bryn Mawr College, Pennsylvania) played Piero in a graduate class production there in 1967: it was directed by Murray Ross. This is the only performance of which I have been able to obtain any record.

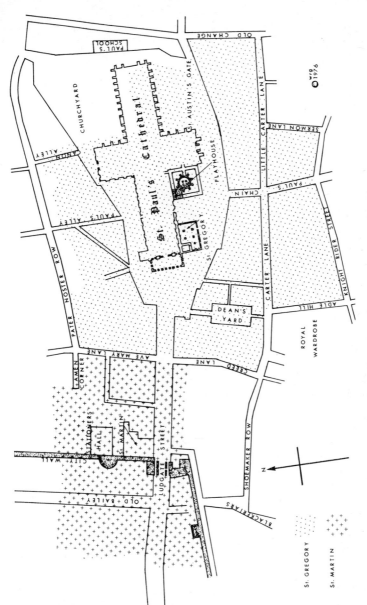

The parishes of St Gregory by Paul's and St Martin Ludgate, 1599–1606

ANTONIO'S REVENGE

[DRAMATIS PERSONAE

Ghost of ANDRUGIO, *late Duke of Genoa.*

*ANTONIO, *his son, betrothed to* MELLIDA.

*PIERO SFORZA, *Duke of Venice.*

GASPAR STROTZO, *his accomplice.*

JULIO, *son to* PIERO.   5

*BALURDO.

*ALBERTO.

*CASTILIO.   } *Gentlemen of the*
                            Venetian Court.
*FOROBOSCO.

PANDULPHO FELICHE.   10

*GALEATZO, *son to the Duke of Florence.*

*MATZAGENTE, *son to the Duke of Milan.*

*LUCIO, *servant to* MARIA.

Two Senators of Venice.

A Herald.   15

Two Mourners.

Four Pages.

Courtiers and Attendants.

D.P.] Bullen, M.S.R., subst.

---

3. PIERO SFORZA] *Cf* Italian *sforzare*, 'to force, to enforce, to constraine, to compell, to ravish'. (Definition(s) from J. Florio, *A Worlde of Wordes, or Dictionarie in Italian and English*, 1598). 'Sforza' was also a common term for a tyrant; a family with this name ruled the Duchy of Milan from 1450 to 1535.

4. GASPAR STROTZO] *strozzare*, 'to wring a sunder, to pull, to tugge or plucke in peeces, to kill or crush to death, to strangle or wring off ones neck'.

6. BALURDO] *balordo*, 'a foole, a noddie, a dizzard, an idiot, a giddiehead'.

8. CASTILIO] In *Antonio and Mellida* he is surnamed BALTHAZAR (III.ii.90.3) as a parody of Baldassare Castiglione, the author of the most famous of Elizabethan courtesy books, *Il Cortegiano* (1528). It is, however, very doubtful whether he is intended to retain this identity in *Antonio's Revenge*.

9. FOROBOSCO] *forabosco*, 'a birde called a Wood-pecker. Also a sneaking prying busie fellow.'

10. PANDULPHO FELICHE] *felice*, 'happie, fortunate, blessed, luckie, prosperous, blissful'.

11. GALEATZO] *galleazza*, 'a galleasse'.

12. MATZAGENTE] *mazza gente*, 'a killer or queller of people, a man queller'.

*MELLIDA, *daughter to* PIERO.

MARIA, *mother to* ANTONIO.

NUTRICHE, *nurse to* MARIA.   20

Two Ladies.]

Those marked * *also appear in* The History of ANTONIO and MELLIDA.
The First Part.

---

20. NUTRICHE] *nutriche, 'a nource, a foster-mother'.* Marston uses the
same device of naming his characters from common Italian words in other
plays, e.g. *The Malcontent* (1603 ?), *The Fawn* (1604 ?), *The Dutch Courtesan*
(1604 ?), as does Jonson in *Volpone, or The Fox* (1606).

ANTONIO'S REVENGE

The Second Part of the History of *Antonio and Mellida.*

The Prologue.

The rawish dank of clumsy winter ramps
The fluent summer's vein; and drizzling sleet

Prol. 1. clumsy] clumzie *Q.*

The Prologue] The intention of this Prologue is to change the setting and mood of the second part of this play from comedy to tragedy (so line 20: the stage was draped in black, a standard Elizabethan device to indicate a tragedy). Marston is following Henryson's advice in *The Testament of Cressid*, 'Ane doolie sessoun to ane cairfull dyte / Suld correspond, and be equivalent' (ll. 1–2). He again uses a description of winter to suit a melancholy tone with the speech of Iacomo in *What You Will*, Wood, II.238, 'The wanton spring lyes dallying with the earth, / ... all things that show or breath, / Are now instaur'd, saving my wretched brest, / That is eternally congeald with Ice / Of froz'd despaire'. This parallelism is, of course, common in Elizabethan poetry, as in Donne's *Twicknam Garden.*

 1. *rawish*]* somewhat raw.

 dank] damp, with the connotation of injurious effect (*O.E.D.*, *a.* 2); *cf.* II.iii.55 and *J. Drum's Ent.*, Wood, III.233, 'The evenings rawe and danke, I shall take cold'.

 clumsy] benumbed or stiffened with cold (*O.E.D.*, *a.* 1); *cf. J. Drum's Ent.*, Wood, III.199, 'clumsie judgements, chilblaind gowtie wits': this usage is parodied by Jonson, '*clumsie chil-blain'd judgement*', and '*clumsie*' is one of the words vomited by Crispinus (*Poet.*, v.iii.286, 485–6).

 ramps]* rises fiercely upon (apparently unique usage as transitive verb). Could mean 'climbs', i.e. 'the humour of winter climbs the vessels where the sap ran free in summer' (see King, p. 13), but it also has the implication of force or savagery, and Hunter glosses, 'snatch, tear, pluck'. Both senses are probably intended. Parodied by Jonson, *Poet.*, v.iii.275–6, '*Rampe up, my* genius; *be not retrograde:* / *But boldly nominate a spade, a spade*': he seems to assume that the word includes the ideas of both 'rising' and 'force'. Marston may have developed his usage from the Italian *rampare*, '*to rampe, to clammer to climbe, to hooke, to dragge*'. The sense is a combination of *O.E.D.*, 'ramp' *vb.*[1] 2 and *vb.*[2] 1.

 2. *fluent*]* flowing (*O.E.D.*, *adj.* 1. *b*); *cf. What You Will*, Wood, II.240, 'O melt thy breath in fluent softer tunes'.

Chilleth the wan bleak cheek of the numbed earth,
Whilst snarling gusts nibble the juiceless leaves
From the naked shudd'ring branch, and pills the skin   5
From off the soft and delicate aspects.
O now, methinks, a sullen tragic scene
Would suit the time with pleasing congruence.
May we be happy in our weak devoir,
And all part pleased in most wished content   10
—But sweat of Hercules can ne'er beget
So blest an issue. Therefore we proclaim,
If any spirit breathes within this round
Uncapable of weighty passion
(As from his birth being huggèd in the arms   15
And nuzzlèd 'twixt the breasts of happiness)
Who winks and shuts his apprehension up

9. devoir] deuoyer Q.

---

3. cheek] Frequently used figuratively; cf. J. Drum's Ent., Wood, III.198,
'grim cheekt night'.

4. snarling gusts]* gusts producing the sound of a snarl (O.E.D., 'snarling'
ppl. a. 3): the phrase is vomited by Crispinus, Poet., v.iii.525.

juiceless]* dried up; cf. What You Will, Wood, II.232, 'some juicles
husk'.

5. pills] strips off the skin (O.E.D., vb.¹ II.5): proverbial, 'Lide pills the
hide' (i.e. March pinches the poor man's beast, Tilley, L.230).

6. aspects] appearances of things.

8. congruence] conformity.

9. May . . . devoir] Although our best effort is not very good, let us hope
that we will be happy with it.

devoir] duty, task.

11. Hercules] lay in one night with forty-nine of the fifty daughters of
Thespius and begot fifty-one sons; the same legend is repeated in Malcontent, IV.v.58–60.

13. round] Cf. 'ring', l. 23 below: amphitheatre, but probably figurative
for theatre; so H5, Prol., 12–14, 'may we cram / Within this wooden O
the very casques / That did affright the air at Agincourt?'. Paul's auditorium could have been semicircular; see frontispiece.

14. Uncapable] Cf. John Webster, The White Devil, 'To the Reader',
21–2, 'the breath that comes from the uncapable multitude'.

16. nuzzlèd] lying snug between; cf. What You Will, Wood, II.263,
'Gowne or Chaine of pearle / Makes my coy minx to nussell twixt the
breastes / Of her lull'd husband'.

17. winks] closes his eyes.

From common sense of what men were, and are,
Who would not know what men must be—let such
Hurry amain from our black-visaged shows;   20
We shall affright their eyes. But if a breast
Nailed to the earth with grief, if any heart
Pierced through with anguish, pant within this ring,
If there be any blood whose heat is choked
And stiflèd with true sense of misery,   25
If ought of these strains fill this consort up,
Th' arrive most welcome. O that our power
Could lackey or keep wing with our desires,
That with unusèd peise of style and sense
We might weigh massy in judicious scale.   30
Yet here's the prop that doth support our hopes:
   When our scenes falter, or invention halts,
   Your favour will give crutches to our faults.   *Exit.*

20. black-visaged] black visag'd *Q*.   29. peise] paize *Q*.

---

20. *black-visaged*] i.e. the stage was draped in black; so *Insatiate C.*, Wood, III.65, 'The stage of heav'n, is hung with solemne black, / A time best fitting to Act Tragedies'.

26. *consort*] harmonious combination of instruments (*O.E.D.*, *sb.*² II.3.*b*).

28. *lackey*] dance attendance upon (*O.E.D.*, *vb.* 2. *trans*).

29. *unusèd*] unusual.

peise] gravity, weight (*O.E.D.*, *sb.* I. *b*): cf. *What You Will*, Wood, II.235, 'To the just skale of even paized thoughts'.

30. *We . . . scale*] (That) what we say may appear substantial to the discriminating spectator.

Act I

Enter PIERO *unbraced, his arms bare, smeared in blood, a poniard in one hand, bloody, and a torch in the other,* STROTZO *following him with a cord.*

Pie. Ho, Gaspar Strotzo, bind Feliche's trunk
    Unto the panting side of Mellida.   [*Exit* STROTZO.]
    'Tis yet dead night; yet all the earth is clutched
    In the dull leaden hand of snoring sleep;
    No breath disturbs the quiet of the air,   5
    No spirit moves upon the breast of earth,
    Save howling dogs, nightcrows, and screeching owls,
    Save meager ghosts, Piero, and black thoughts. [*Clock strikes.*]
    'One, two.' Lord, in two hours what a topless mount

1.i.3. clutched] cloucht *Q.*

---

1. Act and scene division is adhered to as in Q, see Introduction p. 5; the divisions are probably authorial. Marston uses alternation between light and darkness for dramatic effect, see Introduction, p. 35; this scene takes place in darkness, before the court of Piero.

0.1–3.] *Cf. Spanish Tragedy,* III.xii, '*Enter* HIERONIMO *with a poniard in one hand, and a rope in the other.*'

0.1 unbraced] with dress unfastened (*O.E.D.,* ppl. *a.* 1); cf. *What You Will,* Wood, II.237, 'Enter Iacomo unbraced and careles drest'; also Ophelia describes Hamlet's appearance, II.i.78, 'with his doublet all unbrac'd'.

3. *dead night*] time of intensest darkness (*O.E.D.,* 'dead' B. *sb.*¹ 2).

clutched] gripped in the hand (*O.E.D., vb.*¹ 5); cf. v.i.3: the word is vomited by Crispinus (*Poet.,* v.iii.519–22).

4. *snoring*]* that snores (*O.E.D., ppl. a.* 1).

7. *howling*]* that howls (*O.E.D., ppl. a.* 1).

nightcrows] birds of ill omen crying in the night, (?) a nightjar (*O.E.D.*). Jonson mocks the use of these tragic omens, *Poet.,* III.iv.351, '*The dismall night-rauen, and tragicke owle*'.

Of unpeered mischief have these hands cast up!   10

Enter STROTZO.

I can scarce coop triumphing Vengeance up
From bursting forth in braggart passion.
Str. My lord, 'tis firmly said that—
Pie. Andrugio sleeps in peace! This brain hath choked
The organ of his breast. Feliche hangs   15
But as a bait upon the line of death
To 'tice on mischief. I am great in blood,
Unequalled in revenge. You horrid scouts
That sentinel swart night, give loud applause
From your large palms. First know my heart was raised   20
Unto Andrugio's life upon this ground,
Str. Duke, 'tis reported—
Pie. We both were rivals in our May of blood
Unto Maria, fair Ferrara's heir.
He won the Lady, to my honour's death,   25
And from her sweets cropped this Antonio;
For which I burned in inward swelt'ring hate,
And festered rankling malice in my breast,

10.1 S.D.] *so Q; after l. 12 in Hunter.*

---

10. *unpeered*]* unequalled, unrivalled; *cf. I Ant. & Mel.*, v.i.285, 'such
an unpeer'd excellence'.
    11–12. *triumphing . . . passion*] Marston frequently speaks of Vengeance
in a quasi-allegorical or emblematic way, as an anthropomorphic being.
Here the image seems to be that of a caged but potentially violently
demonstrative man; *cf.* II.i.7–8, III.i.45–6, v.i.12 and v.iii.59.
    12. *braggart*]* vainly boastful (*O.E.D.*, B. *adj.*).
    14–15. *This . . . breast*] by my cunning I have killed him.
    16. *line of death*] Feliche hangs like the bait on a fisherman's line. He is
revealed, '*hung up*', at I.iii.129.2.
    17. *'tice*] entice.
    great in blood] It is now 2 a.m.; since midnight Piero has murdered
Andrugio and Feliche.
    18. *scouts*] spies; Piero seems to be referring to the constellations.
    21. *ground*] basis.
    26. *sweets*] embraces; *cf.* IV.iii.188.
    cropped] *Cf. Ant.*, II.ii.232, 'He ploughed her, and she cropp'd'.

Till I might belk revenge upon his eyes.
And now (O blessed now!) 'tis done. Hell, Night,   30
Give loud applause to my hypocrisy.
When his bright valour even dazzled sense
In off'ring his own head, public reproach
Had blurred my name—Speak, Strotzo, had it not?—
If then I had—   35

Str. It had, so please—

Pie. What had, so please? Unseasoned sycophant,
Piero Sforza is no numbèd lord,
Senseless of all true touch; stroke not the head
Of infant speech till it be fully born.   40
Go to!

Str. How now? Fut! I'll not smother your speech.

Pie. Nay, right thine eyes; 'twas but a little spleen.
[*Aside*] Huge plunge!
Sin's grown a slave, and must observe slight evils;   45
Huge villains are enforced to claw all devils.
[*To* STROTZO] Pish! Sweet thy thoughts and give me—

Str. Stroke not the head of infant speech! Go to!

Pie. Nay, calm this storm. I ever held thy breast
More secret and more firm in league of blood   50
Than to be struck in heat with each slight puff.
Give me thy ears. Huge infamy

52–4 Give . . . infamy / Press . . . when / His . . . full,] *so Q;* Give . . .
[had] press['d] down/ My . . . act / Of . . . full, *Bullen.*

---

29. *belk*] belch; *cf.* I.iii.63 and I.iv.6: Elyot's *Dictionary* (1559) defines,
'Eructo . . . *to bealke or breake wynde oute of the stomake.*'

37. *unseasoned*]* not matured by growth or time (*O.E.D.*, *ppl. a.* 2); *cf.*
Poet., v.iii.18–19, 'We have no vacant eare, now, to receiue / The vn-
season'd fruits of his officious tongue' (Jonson uses the word seriously).

44. *plunge*] difficulty, embarrassment. Piero is annoyed at having to
speak fair words to so paltry a rascal as Strotzo (Bullen).

45–6. *Sin's . . . devils*] Sententious or gnomic remarks are often italicised
or set in quotation marks in sixteenth- and seventeenth-century editions.

46. claw] 'Claw-back' was a common term for a sycophant or flatterer.

51. *puff*] brag.

52–5. *Huge . . . head*] Piero is referring to the resurrection scene of *I Ant.
& Mel.*, v.ii; see 'Synopsis of Part I'.

Press down my honour if even then, when
His fresh act of prowess bloomed out full,
I had ta'en vengeance on his hated head.   55
Str. Why it had—
Pie. Could I avoid to give a seeming grant
Unto fruition of Antonio's love ?
Str. No.
Pie. And didst thou ever see a Judas kiss   60
With a more covert touch of fleering hate ?
Str. No.
Pie. And having clipped them with pretence of love
Have I not crushed them with a cruel wring ?
Str. Yes.   65
Pie. Say, faith, didst thou e'er hear, or read, or see
Such happy vengeance, unsuspected death ?
That I should drop strong poison in the bowl
Which I myself caroused unto his health
And future fortune of our unity;   70
That it should work even in the hush of night,
And strangle him on sudden, that fair show
Of death for the excessive joy of his fate
Might choke the murder! Ha, Strotzo, is't not rare ?

71. hush] *Keltie;* husht *Q.*

57–8. *Could . . . love*] How could I avoid giving my apparent consent to
the marriage of Antonio and Mellida ? See 'Synopsis of Part I'.

60. *Judas Kiss*] Proverbial, *cf.* Tilley, 1.92 'To give one a Judas kiss', to
betray.

61. *fleering*] grimacing obsequiously: *cf. Fawn*, II.i.162, 'Come, what are
you fleering at ?'

63. *clipped*] embraced; *cf. Fawn*, I.ii.118–19, 'left it still clipp'd with aged
Neptune's arm'.

68–70. *That . . . unity*] Piero is describing the manner of his murder of
Andrugio; the description seems intended to refer to the last action of
Part I, when Piero calls, 'Fill us fresh wine, the form we'll take by this; /
We'll [Piero and Andrugio] drink a health, while they two [Antonio and
Mellida] sip a kiss' (v.ii.249–50). Andrugio's cup was apparently treated
with a slow-acting poison, like the cup in the duel scene in *Hamlet*, v.ii.

71. *hush*] silence, quiet (*O.E.D.*, 'husht' *sb.*).

74. *choke*] conceal, suppress.

Nay, but weigh it—then Feliche stabbed   75
(Whose sinking thought frightèd my conscious heart)
And laid by Mellida, to stop the match
And hale on mischief. This all in one night!
Is't to be equalled think'st thou ? O, I could eat
Thy fumbling throat for thy lagged censure. Fut!   80
Is't not rare ?
Str.   Yes.
Pie. No! Yes! Nothing but 'no' and 'yes', dull lump ?
Canst thou not honey me with fluent speech
And even adore my topless villainy ?
Will I not blast my own blood for revenge,   85
Must not thou straight be perjured for revenge,
And yet no creature dream 'tis my revenge ?
Will I not turn a glorious bridal morn
Unto a Stygian night ? Yet naught but 'no' and 'yes' ?
Str. I would have told you, if the incubus   90
That rides your bosom would have patience,
It is reported that in private state

81. Is't ... Yes] *so this ed.; two lines Q.*

---

76. *sinking*]* deep discernment, penetrating thought (*O.E.D., ppl. a.* 2. *fig.*). Piero dreaded that his villanies would be detected by Feliche (Bullen).

conscious]* having guilty knowledge (*O.E.D., a.* 4. *b*). Jonson ridicules the attribution of awareness to non-sentient things in *Poet.*, v.iii.287–8, 'bespawles / The conscious time, with humourous fome'. He may be thinking of this Marston context, but a 'heart' can feel, and is thus, in a sense, sentient.

78. *hale*] drag. Jonson ridicules the figurative use of this word; 'doe not exhale me thus', says Crispinus (*Poet.*, III.iii.25) as he is arrested for debt.

80. *lagged censure*]* tardy expression of approval (*O.E.D.*, 'lag' *vb.*[2] 3).

Fut !] An instinctive exclamation—here of exasperation, although *O.E.D.* defines as 'of surprise'.

83. *honey*]* flatter, endear oneself (*O.E.D., vb.* 2).

84. *topless*] unbounded (*O.E.D., a.* 2. *fig.*).

89. *Stygian*]* as black as the river Styx (*O.E.D., a.* 3): the Styx is the most sacred of rivers in the underworld of classical mythology.

90. *incubus*]* the demon of nightmare, and the oppression which results from it (*O.E.D.*, 3). Jonson condemns Marston's metaphorical use of this word, *Poet.*, v.iii.282, 'teach thy incubus to poetize'.

> Maria, Genoa's Duchess, makes to court,
> Longing to see him whom she ne'er shall see,
> Her lord, Andrugio. Belike she hath received   95
> The news of reconciliation
> —Reconciliation with a death!—
> Poor lady shall but find poor comfort in't!

Pie. O, let me swoon for joy. By heaven, I think
     I ha' said my prayers, within this month at least,   100
     I am so boundless happy. Doth she come?
     By this warm reeking gore, I'll marry her.
     Look I not now like an inamorate?
     Poison the father, butcher the son, and marry the mother—ha!
     Strotzo, to bed—snort in securest sleep—   105
     For see, the dapple-gray coursers of the morn
     Beat up the light with their bright silver hooves
     And chase it through the sky. To bed, to bed!
     This morn my vengeance shall be amply fed.   *Exeunt.*

---

106. dapple-gray] dapple gray *Q.*   109. S.D.] *Bullen; Exit Q.*

---

93. *Maria*] Andrugio's widow is evidently unaware of the death of her husband. Marston locates this death during the night that followed the apparent reconciliation at the end of *I Antonio and Mellida*, and it is during the same night that this scene takes place.

96. *reconciliation*] an ironic reference to *I Ant. & Mel.*, v.ii; see 93 n. above.

102. *warm reeking gore*] i.e. the blood of Feliche on his arms and dagger; *cf.* 1.i.75 above.

103. *inamorate*]* a lover; *cf. What You Will*, Wood, 11.250, 'th'inamorate . . . thinkes he sees the absent beauties / Of his lov'd mistress'. Jonson appears to ridicule Marston's extensive use of 'enamoured' as a verb, *cf.* 'I am enamour'd of this street' (Crispinus, *Poet,*. III.i.31). Crispinus vomits three words with the common Marstonian suffix '-ate': '*magnificate*' (v. iii.480), '*inflate*' (v.iii.494), '*fatuate*' (v.iii.499); see King, pp. 18–19.

104. *Poison . . . ha!*] A boast probably derived from Richard of Gloucester's wooing of Anne, *Richard III*, I.ii.229–30, 'I'll have her; but I will not keep her long. / What! I that kill'd her husband and her father—'.

107. *beat up*] drive the game (for hunting), *O.E.D., vb.*[1] 26.

SCENE II.

Enter LUCIO, MARIA and NUTRICHE.

Mar. Stay, gentle Lucio, and vouchsafe thy hand.
Luc. O, Madam!
Mar. Nay, pray thee give me leave to say, 'vouchsafe';
  Submiss entreats beseem my humble state.
  Here let us sit. O, Lucio, fortune's gilt   5
  Is rubbed quite off from my slight tinfoiled state,
  And poor Maria must appear ungraced
  Of the bright fulgor of glossed majesty.
Luc. Cheer up your spirits, madam; fairer chance
  Than that which courts your presence instantly 10
  Cannot be formed by the quick mould of thought.
Mar. Art thou assured the dukes are reconciled?
  Shall my womb's honour wed fair Mellida?
  Will heaven at length grant harbour to my head?
  Shall I once more clip my Andrugio,   15
  And wreathe my arms about Antonio's neck?
  Or is glib rumour grown a parasite,
  Holding a false glass to my sorrow's eyes,
  Making the wrinkled front of grief seem fair,

Scene II] SCENA SECVNDA *Q.*

1.ii. For scene division see Introduction, p. 5; this scene begins at first light and by its end dawn is complete.

 1. *vouchsafe*] condescend to grant (*O.E.D. vb.* 2). The word is used in a context of supplication; Jonson considers it affected when used without a condescending context: 'I pray you, vouchsafe the sight of my armes' (*Poet.*, II.i.94).

 4. *submiss entreats*] humble supplications.

 8. *fulgor*] dazzling brightness or splendour. Marston may have developed this word from the Italian *fulgore, 'a shining, glistring, blazing, or flashing'.*

 10. *courts*] invites you to court (*O.E.D., vb.* 5 and 1).

 presence] appearance before the Duke (in the presence chamber).

 11. *formed . . . thought*] i.e. created by the power of thought, with its speed in conceiving new ideas.

 16. *wreathe*]* wrap (to embrace). Normally means 'fold' (*cf.* I.v.46); (?) this usage is a figurative extension by Marston.

 17. *glib*]* insincere, delusive (*O.E.D., a.* 3): 'Glibbery' (*I Ant. & Mel.*, I.i.108) is vomited by Crispinus (*Poet.*, v.iii.472).

 19. *front*] brow.

Though 'tis much rivelled with abortive care?   20
Luc. Most virtuous princess, banish straggling fear;
       Keep league with comfort, for these eyes beheld
       The dukes united. Yon faint glimmering light
       Ne'er peepèd through the crannies of the east
       Since I beheld them drink a sound carouse   25
       In sparkling Bacchus unto each other's health,
       Your son assured to beauteous Mellida,
       And all clouds cleared of threat'ning discontent.
Mar. What age is morning of?
Luc.   I think 'bout five.
Mar. Nutriche, Nutriche!   30
Nut. Beshrew your fingers! Marry, you have disturbed the
       pleasure of the finest dream. O God, I was even coming
       to it, la. O Jesu, 'twas coming of the sweetest. I'll tell
       you now; methought I was married and methought I
       spent—O Lord, why did you wake me?—and me-   35
       thought I spent three spur-royals on the fiddlers for

26. In . . . health,] *so Bullen;* In . . . Bacchus, / Unto . . . health; *Q.*
29. What . . . five] *so Hunter; two lines Q.*   31. Beshrew] Beshrow *Q.*

---

20. *rivelled*] wrinkled; *cf. Malcontent,* II.iii.68–9, 'grief, that sucks veins
dry, / Rivels the skin'.
abortive] fruitless, useless.
21. *straggling*] hanging back.
23. *glimmering light*] first light of dawn. Marston is at pains to mark the
passage of time in this scene very carefully; see l. 29 below—5 a.m., and
l. 65 below, 'clear day'.
25. *carouse*] *Cf. Ham.,* I.iv.8, 10–11, 'The king doth wake tonight and
takes his rouse, . . . / And, as he drains his draughts of Rhenish down, /
The kettle-drum and trumpet thus bray out'. Later, Piero drinks to music,
v.iv.19 ff.
26. *Bacchus*] god of wine; hence, wine.
27. *assured*] engaged, betrothed (*O.E.D., ppl. a.* A. 3).
31–40.] The bawdy innuendo of Nutriche, about the imagined pleasures
of the wedding night, is ironically contrasted with the chaste and demure
assessment of a wife's duty by Maria (47–61 below).
36. *spur-royals*] Gold coins of 75p value; a star on the reverse resembled
the rowel of a spur: *cf.* Beaumont and Fletcher, *The Scornful Lady,* 'She
has nine *Spur-royals,* and the servants say she hoards old gold' (*Works,* ed.
A. Glover, 1.233).
fiddlers] i.e. employed to play at the wedding.

striking up a fresh hornpipe. Saint Ursula, I was even
going to bed and you—methought, my husband was
even putting out the tapers—when you—Lord, I shall
never have such a dream come upon me as long as—   40
Mar. Peace, idle creature, peace! When will the court rise?
Luc. Madam, 'twere best you took some lodging up,
      And lay in private till the soil of grief
      Were cleared your cheek, and new-burnished lustre
      Clothed your presence, 'fore you saw the dukes   45
      And entered 'mong the proud Venetian states.
Mar. No, Lucio, my dear lord's wise and knows
      That tinsel glitter or rich purfled robes,
      Curled hairs hung full of sparkling carcanets,
      Are not the true adornments of a wife.   50
      So long as wives are faithful, modest, chaste,
      Wise lords affect them. Virtue doth not waste
      With each slight flame of crackling vanity.
      A modest eye forceth affection,

44. new-burnished] new burnisht *Q.*

---

37. *Saint Ursula*] Probably St Ursuline, a legendary British saint;
'. . . invoked here because of her dreams, in which she foresaw her
approaching martyrdom; perhaps also (ironically) because she was the
leader of 11,000 virgins' (Hunter).
   39. *tapers*] candles.
   46. *states*] nobles of Venice.
   47–56.] The sentiments in this speech by Maria appear to be derived
from R. Whyttynton's translation of Seneca's *De Remediis Fortuitorum*
(1547): '*Sensualitie* [i.e. *Feeling*]. I have lost a good wyfe. *Reason.* Thou
shalte fynde as good, yf thou seke nothynge but a good wyfe, all the whyle
thou doest nat regarde her progeny nor her auncestre nor patrimony and
landes whereunto nobilitie it selfe now a dayes inclyneth ,these thynges do
repugne with beaute: thou shalt more easely rule that mynde whiche with
no such vanyte is enhaunsed, the woman is nat fer fro the contempt of her
husbande that setteth overmuche by her selfe' (ed. R. G. Palmer, Chicago,
1953, pp. 63, 65).
   48. *purfled*] embroidered: *cf. Histriom.*, Wood, III.272, 'Ile have a
purfled Roabe'.
   49. carcanets]* a jewelled ornament for the head (*O.E.D.*, 1. *b*).
   52. *affect*] love, honour: *cf.* II.ii.49.
   53. *crackling*] bragging, boastful (*O.E.D.*, *ppl. a.* 2); *cf. What You Will*,
Wood, II.247, 'O this hote crackling love'.

Whilst outward gayness light looks but entice.   55
Fairer than nature's fair is foulest vice.
She that loves art to get her cheek more lovers,
Much outward gauds, slight inward grace, discovers;
I care not to seem fair but to my lord.
Those that strive most to please most strangers' sight,   60
Folly may judge most fair, wisdom most light.

Music sounds a short strain.

But hark, soft music gently moves the air;
I think the bridegroom's up. Lucio, stand close.
O now, Maria, challenge grief to stay
Thy joy's encounter. Look, Lucio, 'tis clear day.   65
[*They remain on stage.*]

SCENE III.

Enter ANTONIO, GALEATZO, MATZAGENTE, BALURDO,
PANDULPHO FELICHE, ALBERTO, CASTILIO *and a Page.*

Ant. Darkness is fled; look, infant morn hath drawn
    Bright silver curtains 'bout the couch of night,
    And now Aurora's horse trots azure rings,

65.1.] *This ed.; They retire to the back of the stage. Bullen.*
Scene III] SCENA TERTIA *Q; not in Bullen, Hunter.*   0.2. ALBERTO'
CASTILIO] *Hunter; Alberto, Forobosco, Castilio Q.*

---

56. *Fairer . . . vice*] To attempt to improve upon one's natural attractive-
ness is morally repulsive: *cf.* the common Renaissance objection to the use
of cometics, e.g. *Ham.*, v.i.188–9, 'let her paint an inch thick, to this favour
[a skull] she must come'.

58. *gauds*] festive finery (*O.E.D.*, *sb.* 2).

61. *light*] immoral.

64–5. *challenge . . . encounter*] i.e. dissipate your grief by the joy of your
reunion with Andrugio and Antonio.

65.1. *They . . . stage*] Lucio, Maria and Nutriche remain on stage but
unseen until I.iii.93, when Maria, recognising Antonio's voice, discloses
herself.

I.iii.2. *curtains*] On the analogy of the curtains around a four-poster bed.

3. *And . . . rings*] 'The horse of the dawn runs around the azure arena
of the sky' (Hunter). Aurora is the goddess of the dawn: to make a horse
tread the ring was an equestrian feat. In Christopher Clifford, *School of*

Breathing fair light about the firmament.
Stand! What's that ?   5
Mat. And if a hornèd devil should burst forth
     I would pass on him with a mortal stock.
Alb. O, a hornèd devil would prove ominous
     Unto a bridegroom's eyes.
Mat. A hornèd devil ? Good, good ; ha, ha, ha! Very good.   10
Alb. Good tanned prince, laugh not. By the joys of love,
     When thou dost girn, thy rusty face doth look
     Like the head of a roasted rabbit ; fie upon't!
Bal. By my troth, methinks his nose is just colour *de roi*.
Mat. I tell thee, fool, my nose will abide no jest.   15
Bal. No, in truth, I do not jest, I speak truth. Truth is the
     touchstone of all things and if your nose will not abide
     the truth, your nose will not abide the touch ; and if your
     nose will not abide the touch, your nose is a copper nose
     and must be nailed up for a slip.   20
Mat. I scorn to retort the obtuse jest of a fool.

     BALURDO *draws out his writing tables and writes.*

12. girn] girne *Q.*

Horsemanship (1585), directions are given for 'trotting the great ring, and
what order is to be observed therein' (Bullen).
     6. *And if*] even if.
     7. *stock*] a thrust in fencing (*O.E.D.*, *sb.*³ 2).
     8. *hornèd devil*] i.e. a herald of the cuckold's horns.
     11. *tanned*] sunburnt: see also 'rusty', 12 below. This is perhaps an
indication that the boys were using cosmetics for make-up.
     12. *girn*] grin (*O.E.D.*, *vb.*¹ 2).
     14. *colour* de roi] Cotgrave, *A Dictionarie of the French and English
Tongues* (1611), declares, 'Couleur de roy. *A title in old time due onely unto
Purple, though usurped at this day by a kind of bright Tawnie, which we also
tearme de roy colour*' (i.e. orange-brown).
     18. *touch*] i.e. the test for true gold, determined by applying a touchstone
(here 'of truth').
     20. *slip*] counterfeit coin (i.e. copper washed over with gold): *cf. I Ant.
& Mel.*, v.ii.22–3, 'make me a slip and let me go but for ninepence'. When
detected, slips were nailed to a shop counter (Bullen).
     21.1. *writing tables*] notebooks: *cf. Ham.*, I.v.107, 'My tables—meet it is
I set it down'.

Bal. 'Retort' and 'obtuse'; good words, very good words.

Gal. Young prince, look sprightly; fie, a bridegroom sad!

Bal. In truth, if he were retort and obtuse, no question he
    would be merry; but, and please my Genius, I will be   25
    most retort and obtuse ere night. I'll tell you what I'll
    bear soon at night in my shield for my device.

Gal. What, good Balurdo?

Bal. O, do me right; Sir Geoffrey Balurdo—Sir, Sir, as long
    as ye live, Sir.   30

Gal. What, good Sir Geoffrey Balurdo?

Bal. Marry, forsooth, I'll carry for my device my grand-
    father's great stone-horse flinging up his head and jerk-
    ing out his left leg; the word, *Wighy Purt*. As I am a true
    knight, will't not be most retort and obtuse, ha?   35

Ant. Blow hence these sapless jests. I tell you bloods
    My spirit's heavy, and the juice of life
    Creeps slowly through my stiffened arteries.
    Last sleep my sense was steeped in horrid dreams:

---

34. *Wighy Purt*] *Q; Weehee Purt Hunter.*

---

22. *'retort' . . . 'obtuse'*] Cf. *'endear'* and *'intimate'*, II.i.48: this affectation
of Balurdo to write down new words is a means whereby Marston draws
attention to his vividly contemporary and original vocabulary. In *Scourge
Vil.*, XI.37–51, Marston had already mocked this affectation in one *Luscus*,
who 'H'ath made a common-place booke out of plaies, / And speakes
in print, at least what ere he sayes / Is warranted by Curtaine *plaudeties*'
(ll. 43–5).

25. *and*] and if it.

27. *device*] heraldic design: in *I Ant. & Mel.*, V.i.20–2, there is a mock
knighting ceremony for Balurdo, and there he claims for his device, 'a good
fat leg of ewe mutton swimming in stew'd broth of plums', with the motto
'Hold my dish whilst I spill my pottage': see also V.ii.10–12 below.

29. *do me right*] Balurdo is referring to his song in *I Ant. & Mel.*, V.ii.26,
'Do me right, and dub me knight'; see 66 n. below.

33. *stone-horse*] a stallion.

34. *word*] motto.

Wighy Purt] i.e. the neighing of a horse. The whole phrase may mean
'a sulky nay', with a pun on 'neigh' and 'nay' (i.e. a petulant refusal).

36. *sapless*]* insipid, trivial.

bloods] gallants.

Three parts of night were swallowed in the gulf   40
Of ravenous time when to my slumbr'ing powers
Two meager ghosts made apparition.
The one's breast seemed fresh-paunched with bleeding
     wounds
Whose bubbling gore sprang in frighted eyes:
The other ghost assumed my father's shape;   45
Both cried, 'Revenge!' At which my trembling joints
(Icèd quite over with a frozed cold sweat)
Leaped forth the sheets. Three times I gasped at shades,
And thrice, deluded by erroneous sense,
I forced my thoughts make stand; when, lo, I oped   50
A large bay window, through which the night
Struck terror to my soul. The verge of heaven
Was ringed with flames and all the upper vault
Thick-laced with flakes of fire; in midst whereof
A blazing comet shot his threat'ning train   55
Just on my face. Viewing these prodigies,
I bowed my naked knee and pierced the star
With an outfacing eye, pronouncing thus:

40. parts] *1633;* parrs *Q.*   43. fresh-paunched] fresh pauncht *Q.*
48. gasped] *Q;* grasp'd *Keltie, Bullen, Hunter.*   54. Thick-laced] Thick
lac't *Q.*

40–6. *Three . . . Revenge*] Perhaps this is an echo of the action in the lost
Ur-Hamlet; see Introduction, p. 18.

42. *Two meager ghosts*] i.e. Feliche and Andrugio.

43. *fresh-paunched*] newly punctured: in *Poet.* (Q only), III.iv.173, Tucca
addresses Histrio as 'Paunch'.

45.] Cf. *Ham.,* I.ii.243, 'If it assume my noble father's person'.

46–50.] A reminiscence of Virgil, *Aeneid,* III.174–5 and VI.699–700
(Bullen): 'Chill sweat spread over me. I started from my bed . . . Three
times he tried to cast his arms about his father's neck' (trans. Jackson
Knight).

48. *gasped*] Bullen's emendation, followed by Hunter, makes good sense
but so does the Q reading.

50. *I . . . stand*] I forced myself to regain my composure.

55. *blazing comet*] an evil omen; so F. Nausea, *A Treatise of Blazing
Starres* (1618), 'Comets carry with them a Prognostication of some strange
wonder . . . they threaten some eminent evill and mischiefe' (*sig.* C3v).

58. *outfacing*] outstaring, undaunted.

Deus imperat astris. At which my nose straight bled!
Then doubled I my word, so slunk to bed.   60

Bal. Verily, Sir Geoffrey had a monstrous strange dream the
last night. For methought I dreamt I was asleep, and
methought the ground yawned and belked up the
abominable ghost of a misshapen Simile, with two ugly
pages, the one called Master *Even-as,* going before, and   65
the other Mounser *Even-so,* following after, whilst
Signior Simile stalked most prodigiously in the midst.
At which I bewrayed the fearfulness of my nature, and
—being ready to forsake the fortress of my wit—start
up, called for a clean shirt, eat a mess of broth, and with 70
that I awaked.

Ant. I pray thee peace. I tell you gentlemen
The frightful shades of night yet shake my brain;
My gellied blood's not thawed; the sulphur damps
That flow in wingèd lightning 'bout my couch   75

65–6. Master *Even-as,* ... Mounser *Even-so,*] *Wood;* master, even as going
before; and the other *Mounser,* even so *Q.*   72. pray thee] *Hunter;* pree
thee *Q;* prithee *Bullen.*

---

59. Deus ... astris] God rules the stars.
nose ... bled] an evil omen.
60. *doubled . . . word*] i.e. repeated 'God rules the stars', to reassure
myself.
66. *Mounser*] i.e. Monsieur. There may be another echo here of Balurdo's
song from *I Ant. & Mel.,* v.ii.26–7, which is a version of the concluding
phrase of the catch 'Mousieur (or Monser) Mingo', based on Orlando di
Lasso's 'Un jour vis un foulon' (published in *Mellange,* 1570). The same
song occurs in *2H4,* v.iii.73–5, with 'Samingo' in place of 'Balurdo'. See
F. W. Sternfeld, 'Lasso's music for Shakespeare's 'Samingo', *Sh.Q.,* 9
(1958) 105–16.
68. *bewrayed*] i.e. both 'befouled myself' and 'betrayed my fear'; *cf.*
Middleton, *Blurt, Master Constable,* IV.iii.151–3. '*Blurt.* Your being in
your shirt bewrays you [i.e. befoul]. / *Lazarillo.* I beseech thee, most honest
Blurt, let not my shirt bewray me [i.e. betray]': a combination of *O.E.D.,*
'bewray' *vb.* 6 and 'beray' *vb.* 1.
74. *gellied*]* frozen. This is probably an adjective formed by a conflation
of 'geal', to congeal and 'gelid', cold as ice (*O.E.D., a.* 1).
damps]* fog, mist (*O.E.D., sb.*[1] 2. *fig.*). Crispinus vomits the phrase
'conscious damp' (*Poet.,* v.iii.506).

Yet stick within my sense, my soul is great
In expectation of dire prodigies.

Pan. Tut, my young prince, let not thy fortunes see
Their lord a coward. He that's nobly born
Abhors to fear; base fear's the brand of slaves,   80
He that observes, pursues, slinks back for fright,
Was never cast in mould of noble spright.

Gal. Tush, there's a sun will straight exhale these damps
Of chilling fear. Come, shall's salute the bride?

Ant. Castilio, I prithee mix thy breath with his.   85
Sing one of Signior Renaldo's airs
To rouse the slumb'ring bride from gluttoning
In surfeit of superfluous sleep. Good signior, sing.

They [GALEATZO *and* CASTILIO] *sing.*

What means this silence and unmovèd calm?
Boy, wind thy cornet; force the leaden gates   90
Of lazy sleep fly open with thy breath.
My Mellida not up? not stirring yet? umh!

Mar. That voice should be my son's, Antonio's.
Antonio!

85. prithee] *Bullen*; pree the *Q;* pray thee *Hunter.*   88.1.] *This ed.;*
CANTANT *Q; A Song Bullen; Cantant* [Galeatzo *and* Castilio] *Hunter.*

---

76. *great*]* pregnant; *cf. I Ant. & Mel.*, I.i.165, 'Our pregnant thoughts,
even great of much desire' (*O.E.D., a.* 3. *b. fig.*).

83. *sun*] Mellida.

exhale] evaporate: see I.i.78 n.

84. *salute the bride*] The traditional dawn song, or aubade, to the bride
on the morning of the wedding: so Spenser, *Epithalamion*, 'Helpe me mine
owne loves praises to resound' (1. 14.)

85. *his*] i.e. sing with Galeatzo.

86. *Signior Renaldo*] In the *Faerie Queene* Spenser speaks of 'that same
water of Ardenne, / The which *Rinaldo* drunck in happie howre', IV iii.
45.2–3; the effect was to change hate into love (the story is derived from
Ariosto). The change from previous misfortune and enmity to love and
rejoicing is appropriate to the play at this point.

Hunter suggests that the Paduan Giulio Renaldi (*fl.* 1569) may be
specifically intended. Polonius' servant who is sent to inquire of Laertes'
behaviour in Paris is named Reynaldo, and Polonius' last injunction to
him is 'And let him [Laertes] ply his music' (*Ham.*, II.i.73).

90. *wind*] play.

Ant. Here. Who calls ? Here stands Antonio.   95
Mar. Sweet son!
Ant.   Dear mother!
Mar. Fair honour of a chaste and loyal bed,
     Thy father's beauty, thy sad mother's love,
     Were I as powerful as the voice of fate,
     Felicity complete should sweet thy state;   100
     But all the blessings that a poor banished wretch
     Can pour upon thy head, take, gentle son;
     Live, gracious youth, to close thy mother's eyes,
     Loved of thy parents till their latest hour.
     How cheers my lord, thy father ? O sweet boy,   105
     Part of him thus I clip, my dear, dear joy.
                              [*Embraces* ANTONIO.]
Ant. Madam, last night I kissed his princely hand,
     And took a treasured blessing from his lips.
     O mother, you arrive in jubilee,
     And firm atonement of all boist'rous rage: 110
     Pleasure, united love, protested faith,
     Guard my loved father as sworn pensioners;
     The dukes are leagued in firmest bond of love
     And you arrive even in the solsticy
     And highest point of sunshine happiness.   115

               One winds a cornet within.

     Hark, madam, how yon cornet jerketh up
     His strained shrill accents in the capering air,

96. Sweet . . . mother!] *so this ed.; two lines Q.*

---

     103. *close . . . eyes*] The last duty of child to parent.
     105. *cheers*] fares.
     109. *jubilee*] season of joyful celebration (*O.E.D.*, *sb.* 4).
     110. *atonement of*] reconciliation after.
112. *sworn pensioners*] i.e. guards paid by the Duke and sworn to protect
him.
     114. *solsticy*] crisis point or furthest limit; the summer and winter solstice
(21 June and 22 December) are the days when the sun is furthest from the
equator.

As proud to summon up my bright-cheeked love.
Now, mother, ope wide expectation,
Let loose your amplest sense, to entertain   120
Th' impression of an object of such worth
That life's too poor to—
Gal. Nay, leave hyperboles.
Ant. I tell thee, prince, that presence straight appears
Of which thou canst not form hyperboles;   125
The trophy of triumphing excellence
The heart of beauty, Mellida, appears.
See, look, the curtain stirs; shine nature's pride,
Love's vital spirit, dear Antonio's bride!

The curtain's drawn and the body of FELICHE, *stabbed
thick with wounds, appears hung up.*

What villain bloods the window of my love?   130
What slave hath hung yon gory ensign up,
In flat defiance of humanity?
Awake, thou fair unspotted purity,
Death's at thy window! Awake, bright Mellida!
Antonio calls.   135

---

118. bright-cheeked] bright cheek't *Q*.

---

129. 1–2] *Cf. Spanish Tragedy*, II.iv, '*They hang him* [HORATIO] *in the arbour . . . They stab him . . . Exeunt* [, *leaving* HORATIO'*s body*]' (53, 55, 63.1). Later, at IV.iv.88, Hieronimo discloses the body of his dead son, Horatio. A similar revelation occurs in the opening lines of Chettle's *Hoffman* (1602 ?), I.i.6.1, where Hoffman '*strikes ope a curtaine where appeares a body*'. An even closer parallel to this situation is found in Middleton's *Blurt, Master Constable* (1601–2), where Camillo and Virgilio plan to capture Fontinelle at the 'strumpet Imperia's ' and 'found, to kill him— / *Vir.* And killed, to hang out his reeking body at his harlot's window' (v.i.27, 29–31).

130. *window*] The implication here (and at 134 below) is that Feliche's body was hung behind a curtain which was, in turn, inside a window and thus, probably, at one side of the 'above'; see Introduction, p. 28.

131. *ensign*] banner. Jonson mocks the metaphorical use of this word in *Cynthia Revels*, 'Lady, vouchsafe the tenure of this ensigne' (Amorphus, V.iv.140–1).

SCENE IV.

Enter PIERO *as at first, with* FOROBOSCO.

Pie. Who gives these ill-befitting attributes
    Of chaste, unspotted, bright to Mellida,
    He lies as loud as thunder; she's unchaste,
    Tainted, impure, black as the soul of hell.

ANTONIO *draws his rapier, offers to run at*
PIERO, *but* MARIA *holds his arm and stays him.*

Ant. Dog, I will make thee eat thy vomit up,   5
    Which thou hast belked 'gainst taintless Mellida.
Pie. Ram't quickly down, that it may not rise up
    To embraid my thoughts. Behold my stomach's—
    Strike me quite through with the relentless edge
    Of raging fury. Boy I'll kill thy love.   10
    Pandulph Feliche, I have stabbed thy son;
    Look, yet his lifeblood reeks upon this steel.
    Albert, yon hangs thy friend. Have none of you
    Courage of vengeance? Forget I am your Duke;
    Think Mellida is not Piero's blood;   15
    Imagine on slight ground I'll blast his honour;
    Suppose I saw not that incestuous slave
    Clipping the strumpet with luxurious twines!
    O, numb my sense of anguish, cast my life
    In a dead sleep whilst law cuts off yon maim,   20
    Yon putrid ulcer of my royal blood.

Scene IV] SCENA QVARTA *Q; not in Bullen, Hunter.*   4.1. ANTONIO]
1633; He Q.   7. S. H. *Pie.*] *1633; not in Q.*   20. maim] *1633;* maine *Q.*

    I.iv.0.I. as at first] i.e. as in I.i.0.1–2, '*unbraced, his arms bare, smeared
in blood, a poniard in one hand bloody ,and a torch in the other* . . .'
    I. *Who*] whoever.
    8. *embraid*] upbraid; cf. *Malcontent,* IV.iii.132–3, 'their presence still /
Imbraids our fortunes'.
    16. *his*] Antonio's.
    17. *incestuous slave*] lecherous villain.
    18. *luxurious twines*]* lustful embraces (*O.E.D.,* 'twines' *sb.*[1] 3).
    20. *maim*] blemish, defect.

For. Keep league with reason, gracious sovereign.
Pie. There glow no sparks of reason in the world,
  All are raked up in ashy beastliness;
  The bulk of man's as dark as Erebus,   25
  No branch of reason's light hangs in his trunk;
  There lives no reason to keep league withal,
  I ha' no reason to be reasonable.
  Her wedding eve, linked to the noble blood
  Of my most firmly reconcilèd friend,   30
  And found even clinged in sensuality!
  O heaven! O heaven! Were she as near my heart
  As is my liver, I would rend her off.

Scene V.
Enter STROTZO.

Str. Whither, O whither shall I hurl vast grief?
Pie. Here, into my breast; 'tis a place built wide
  By fate to give receipt to boundless woes.
Str. O no; here throb those hearts which I must cleave
  With my keen piercing news. Andrugio's dead.   5
Pie. Dead?
Mar.   O me most miserable!
Pie. Dead! alas, how dead?
  [*Aside*] Fut, weep, act, feign.
      Gives seeming passion.
         Dead! alas, how dead?
Str. The vast delights of his large sudden joys
  Opened his powers so wide, that's native heat   10
  So prodigally flowed t'exterior parts
  That th' inner citadel was left unmanned,

Scene v] SCENA QVINTA *Q; not in Keltie, Bullen, Hunter.* 6. Dead . . .
miserable!] *so this ed.; two lines Q.* 8. S.D.] *after l. 7 in Q.* 12.
th'inner] *Bullen;* thinner *Q.*

---

 25. *Erebus*] Hell. In *Poet.*, III.iv, Jonson satirises the language of tragedy,
including the phrase '*princely* EREBVS' (257).
 26. *branch*] arm of a chandelier (*O.E.D., sb.* 2. *d*).

And so surprised on sudden by cold death.

Mar. O, fatal, disastrous, cursèd, dismal!
Choke breath and life. I breathe, I live too long,   15
Andrugio, my lord, I come, I come. [*Swoons.*]

Pie. Be cheerful, princess; help, Castilio,
The lady's swooned; help to bear her in.
Slow comfort to huge cares is swiftest sin.

Bal. Courage, courage, sweet lady; 'tis Sir Geoffrey Balurdo   20
bids you courage. Truly I am as nimble as an elephant
about a lady.

[*Exeunt* PIERO, FOROBOSCO, CASTILIO *and* BALURDO,
LUCIO *and* NUTRICHE, *bearing out* MARIA.]

Pan. Dead!

Ant.   Dead!

Alb.   Dead!

Ant. Why now the womb of mischief is delivered
Of the prodigious issue of the night.   25

Pan. Ha, ha, ha.

Ant. My father dead, my love attaint of lust,
(That's a large lie, as vast as spacious hell!),
Poor guiltless lady—O accursèd lie!
What, whom, whither, which shall I first lament?   30
A dead father, a dishonoured wife? Stand!
Methinks I feel the frame of nature shake.
Cracks not the joints of earth to bear my woes?

22.1–2.] *Bullen.*

I.v.19. *Slow . . . sin*] 'It is a speedy kind of sinfulness to bring relief
slowly to those who have suffered greatly' (Hunter).

25. *prodigious*] monstrous, horrible; especially applied to birth; *cf. R3*,
I.ii.22.

26. *Ha, ha, ha.*] The same ironic laughter is uttered by Titus after he has
been presented by Marcus with the severed heads of his sons, *Tit.*,
III.i.265.

32. *frame of nature*] i.e. the disturbance in the microcosm (man) is
reflected by the disruption in the macrocosm (the universe or nature at
large); *cf. Lr.*, III.i.10–11, 'Strives in his little world of man to out-scorn /
The to-and-fro conflicting wind and rain'.

Alb. Sweet prince, be patient.

Ant. 'Slid, sir, I will not, in despite of thee.   35
    Patience is slave to fools, a chain that's fixed
    Only to posts and senseless log-like dolts.

Alb. 'Tis reason's glory to command affects.

Ant. Lies thy cold father dead, his glossèd eyes
    New closèd up by thy sad mother's hands?   40
    Hast thou a love as spotless as the brow
    Of clearest heaven, blurred with false defames?
    Are thy moist entrails crumpled up with grief
    Of parching mischief? Tell me, does thy heart
    With punching anguish spur thy gallèd ribs?   45
    Then come, and let's sit and weep and wreathe our arms;
    I'll hear thy counsel.

Alb.   Take comfort.

Ant. Confusion to all comfort! I defy it.
    Comfort's a parasite, a flatt'ring Jack,
    And melts resolved despair. O boundless woe,   50
    If there be any black yet unknown grief,
    If there be any horror yet unfelt,
    Unthought of mischief in thy fiendlike power,

---

35. '*Slid*] God's lid, i.e. eyelid; a common form of oath; *cf*. IV.v.54.

37. *log-like*]* torpid (*O.E.D.*, *sb.*¹ 8. *d*).

38. *affects*] passions (i.e. it is the great virtue of man's power of reasoning that he can use it to control his emotions). This is, of course, a Renaissance commonplace; so Richard Hooker, 'Appetite is the Will's solicitor, and the Will is Appetite's controller; what we covet according to the one by the other we often reject; neither is any other desire termed properly Will, but that where Reason and Understanding, or the show of Reason, prescribeth the thing desired' (*The Laws of Ecclesiastical Polity*, 1593; Everyman edn., I, 170).

39. *glossèd*] glazed; *cf*. I.ii.8.

42. *blurred*]* defiled; *cf. I Ant. & Mel.*, I.i.211, 'blurr'd the jocund face of bright-cheek'd day'.

44–5. *does . . . ribs*] i.e. does your heart beat against your chafed ribs with stabbing grief? The metaphor is taken from spurring a horse: *cf. Mac.*, I.iii.136, 'And make my seated heart knock at my ribs'.

46. *wreathe*] fold (in friendship).

49. *Jack*] a knave; *cf. R3*, I.iii.52–3, 'abus'd / With silken, sly, insinuating Jacks'.

Dash it upon my miserable head,
Make me more wretch, more cursèd if thou canst.   55
O, now my fate is more than I could fear,
My woes more weighty than my soul can bear.   *Exit.*
Pan. Ha, ha, ha.
Alb. Why laugh you, uncle? That's my coz, your son,
Whose breast hangs casèd in his cluttered gore.   60
Pan. True, man, true; why, wherefore should I weep?
Come sit, kind nephew; come on; thou and I
Will talk as chorus to this tragedy.
Entreat the music strain their instruments
With a slight touch whilst we—Say on, fair coz.   65
Alb. He was the very hope of Italy,

Music sounds softly.

The blooming honour of your drooping age.
Pan. True, coz, true. They say that men of hope are crushed,
Good are suppressed by base desertless clods,
That stifle gasping virtue. Look, sweet youth,   70
How provident our quick Venetians are
Lest hooves of jades should trample on my boy;
Look how they lift him up to eminence,
Heave him 'bove reach of flesh. Ha, ha, ha.
Alb. Uncle, this laughter ill becomes your grief.   75
Pan. Wouldst have me cry, run raving up and down

---

57. *Ha, ha, ha*] See l. 26 above.
60. *cluttered*] coagulated; *cf. J. Drum's Ent.*, Wood, III.201, 'bake in thy cluttered bloud': Cotgrave speaks of 'Grumeau de sang, *a clot or clutter of congealed bloud*'.
64. *the music*] i.e. the musicians in the gallery above.
65. *a slight touch*] i.e. a gentle sound.
69. *desertless*]* undeserving (*O.E.D.*, *a.*[1] 1).
Good . . . clods] Good men are weighed down by worthless louts.
72. *jades*] worn-out old horses.
boy] i.e. Feliche, whose body remains visible, 'hung up', from I.iii. 129.1–2 until the end of Act I.
74. *Ha, ha, ha*] see l. 26 and l. 57 above.
76–9.] He refuses to behave like Hieronimo in *The Spanish Tragedy*, III.vii.1–4, 'Where shall I run to breathe abroad my woes, / My woes,

For my son's loss ? Wouldst have me turn rank mad,
Or wring my face with mimic action,
Stamp, curse, weep, rage, and then my bosom strike ?
Away, 'tis apish action, player-like. 80
If he is guiltless, why should tears be spent ?
Thrice blessèd soul that dieth innocent.
If he is lepered with so foul a guilt,
Why should a sigh be lent, a tear be spilt ?
The gripe of chance is weak to wring a tear 85
From him that knows what fortitude should bear.
Listen, young blood, 'tis not true valour's pride
To swagger, quarrel, swear, stamp, rave and chide,
To stab in fume of blood, to keep loud coil,
To bandy factions in domestic broils, 90
To dare the act of sins whose filth excels

---

whose weight hath wearied the earth ? / Or mine exclaims, that have
surcharg'd the air / With ceaseless plaints for my deceased son ?' and in
The Malcontent, IV.iv.4, Malevole warns Pietro not to become like
Hieronimo, 'O, do not rand, do not turn player'; Hamlet gives a similar
warning to the players who arrive at Elsinore, 'O, it offends me to the soul
to hear a robustious periwig-pated fellow tear a passion to tatters, to very
rags' (III.ii.11–13).

77. rank]* completely (O.E.D., c. adv. 2); cf. What You Will, Wood,
II.238, 'he's irrecoverable, mad, ranke madde'.
78. wring] distort.
mimic action]* exaggerated gestures (O.E.D., 'mimic' a. 2. b).
80. apish] unintelligent imitation. This speech appears to be an attack
by Marston upon what he alleges to be the style of acting in the public
playhouses.
83. lepered] diseased (as with leprosy), foully infected.
85. gripe] clutch (with the implication of causing distress), O.E.D., sb.[1]
2; cf. II.v.7.
88. chide] brawl, wrangle.
89. stab] murder.
fume] smoke, heat; cf. Cynthia's Revels, I.iii.43–4, 'the least steame, or
fume of a reason'. Jonson may be mocking the usage, as the phrase is used
by Amorphus in an affected manner.
keep loud coil] i.e. cause a noisy disturbance; cf. Spanish Tragedy,
III.xiii.45, 'How now, what noise ? What coil is that you keep ?'
90. bandy factions] wrangle in partisan causes; cf. 1H6, IV.i.190, 'This
factious bandying of their favourites'.

    The blackest customs of blind infidels.
    No, my loved youth, he may of valour vaunt
    Whom fortune's loudest thunder cannot daunt,
    Whom fretful galls of chance, stern fortune's siege   95
    Makes not his reason slink, the soul's fair liege,
    Whose well-peised action ever rests upon
    Not giddy humours, but discretion.
    This heart in valour even Jove out-goes;
    Jove is without, but this 'bove sense of woes;   100
    And such a one, eternity. Behold!   [*Pointing to* FELICHE.]
    Good morrow, son; thou bid'st a fig for cold.
    Sound louder music; let my breath exact
    You strike sad tones unto this dismal act.   [*Exeunt.*]

95. galls] *1633;* gaules *Q*.   97. well-peised] *Hunter;* well pais'd *Q*.
101. eternity. Behold! . . . FELICHE] *so this ed.;* eternitie: Behold, *Q;*
eternity. Behold—*Keltie;* eternity. [*To* Feliche.] Behold *Hunter*.

---

   92. *blind*] without the light of the Gospel.
   95. *fretful galls*] i.e. sores caused by rubbing. Marston's 'gaules' (Q) may
also include the idea of the wind of fortune (i.e. gales).
   96. *slink*] cower.
   leige] i.e. of reason, which should rule the soul.
   97. *well-peised*] responsibly decided, carefully weighed.
   98. *giddy humours*] irrational emotions.
   discretion] This has four syllables.
   99–101. *This . . . eternity*] A free rendering of a quotation from Seneca's
De Providentia, VI.6, which occurs at II.iii.45–8. 'My heart is braver than
Jove's, Jove does not experience human feeling, but I have raised myself
above it while remaining conscious of it, and thus I have become one with
the eternal.'
   102. *bid'st a fig*] art indifferent to.
   103. *exact*] require with authority.
   104. *act*] (i) of the play and (ii) of beholding the body of Feliche.

Act II

SCENE I.

The cornets sound a sennet.

Enter two mourners with torches, two with streamers, CASTILIO *and*
FOROBOSCO *with torches, a Herald bearing Andrugio's helm and
sword, the coffin,* MARIA *supported by* LUCIO *and* ALBERTO,
ANTONIO *by himself,* PIERO *and* STROTZO *talking,* GALEATZO
and MATZAGENTE, BALURDO *and* PANDULPHO; *the coffin set
down, helm, sword, and streamers hung up, placed by the Herald,
whilst* ANTONIO *and* MARIA *wet their handkerchiefs with their tears,
kiss them, and lay them on the hearse, kneeling. All go out but*
PIERO. *Cornets cease and he speaks.*

Pie. Rot there, thou cerecloth that enfolds the flesh
    Of my loathed foe; moulder to crumbling dust;
    Oblivion choke the passage of thy fame!
    Trophies of honoured birth drop quickly down;
    Let naught of him, but what was vicious, live.   5
    Though thou art dead, think not my hate is dead;
    I have but newly twone my arm in the curled locks

   II. This act takes place inside the court of Piero, during the day following the dawn described in act I.

   0.1. cornets . . . sennet.] Horns sound a set of notes as a signal for the
opening of the act, as frequently in Elizabethan drama; *cf.* opening stage
directions for later acts and several other scenes of this play.

   0.2. streamers] pennons.

   1. *cerecloth*] winding-sheet.

   enfolds]* wraps up.

   7. *twone*] twined.

   7–8. *curled . . . snaky vengeance*] Probably an allusion to the Hydra of the
Lernaean Spring, represented in Greek mythology as having nine snake-
like heads, each of which, being cut off, was immediately replaced by two
new ones unless the wound was cauterised. The destruction of this monster
was one of the twelve labours of Hercules; *cf.* I.i.11–12 and III.i.45–6.

Of snaky Vengeance. Pale beetle-browed hate
But newly bustles up. Sweet wrong, I clap thy thoughts.
O, let me hug my bosom, rub my breast,   10
In hope of what may hap. Andrugio rots,
Antonio lives; umh; how long? ha, ha, how long?
Antonio packed hence, I'll his mother wed,
Then clear my daughter of supposèd lust,
Wed her to Florence' heir. O, excellent!   15
Venice, Genoa, Florence at my beck,
At Piero's nod—Balurdo, O, ho,—
O, 'twill be rare, all unsuspected done.
I have been nursed in blood, and still have sucked
The steam of reeking gore. Balurdo, ho!   20

Enter BALURDO *with a beard half off, half on.*

Bal. When my beard is on, most noble prince, when my
      beard is on.
Pie. Why, what dost thou with a beard?
Bal. In truth, one told me that my wit was bald and that a
      mermaid was half fish, and half fish; and therefore to   25

II.i.10. my bosom . . . my breast] *Q;* thy bosome . . . thy breast *1633.*
20.1. *off*] *1633; of Q.*   25. and half fish] *Q;* and half flesh *Halliwell,*
Keltie, Wood.

---

8. *beetle-browed*] scowling, sullen, lowering.
9. *bustles up*] bestirs itself (with fuss and commotion).
clap] applaud.
10. *hug*]* congratulate oneself (*O.E.D., vb.* 2. *b fig.*): see Cross, *N. &*
Q., 204, 255.
13. *I'll his mother wed*] see I.i.104 n.
17.] Bullen notes, 'We are to suppose that Piero has left the church and
is in the courtyard of the palace,' and Sir E. K. Chambers accepts this
explanation of the action (*Elizabethan Stage,* III.140). There does not,
however, appear to be any carefully indicated and detailed location given
other than a general overall impression in Act I of 'outside' and in Act II of
'inside'.
20. *reeking*] Cf. 'the smoake of reeking bloud', *J. Drum's Ent.,* Wood,
III.232.
20.1] Cf. *The Spanish Tragedy,* IV.iii.18–19, '*Hieronimo* (to Balthazar) . .
is your beard on? / *Bal.* Half on, the other is in my hand'. See Introduction, p. 38.

speak wisely, like one of your council, as indeed it hath
pleased you to make me, not only, being a fool, of your
council, but also to make me of your council, being a
fool. If my wit be bald and a mermaid be half fish and
half conger, then I must be forced to conclude—the   30
tiring man hath not glued on my beard half fast enough.
God's bores, it will not stick to fall off.

Pie. Dost thou know what thou hast spoken all this while?

Bal. O Lord, Duke, I would be sorry of that. Many men can
utter that which no man but themselves can conceive;   35
but I thank a good wit, I have the gift to speak that
which neither any man else nor myself understands.

Pie. Thou art wise. He that speaks he knows not what shall
never sin against his own conscience; go to, thou art
wise.   40

Bal. Wise? O no; I have a little natural discretion or so; but
for wise—I am somewhat prudent; but for wise—O
Lord!

Pie. Hold, take those keys, open the castle vault and put in
Mellida.   45

Bal. And put in Mellida? well, let me alone.

Pie. Bid Forobosco and Castilio guard;
Endear thyself Piero's intimate.

Bal. 'Endear' and 'intimate'—good, I assure you. I will
endear and intimate Mellida into the dungeon presently.   50

Pie. Will Pandulpho Feliche wait on me?

Bal. I will make him come, most retort and obtuse, to you

---

30. *conger*] an eel.

32. *God's bores*] God's (i.e. Christ's) wounds.

48. *Endear*] win the affection of (Piero). Here Marston appears to be
mocking gallants who took this word seriously; Jonson also condemns its
use, *cf. Poet.*, Crispinus, III.iv.80, 'you do most infinitely endeare, and
oblige me to you': later, at II.iii.28, Marston uses it seriously.

intimate]* a very close friend or associate (*O.E.D.*, *sb.* 3); *cf.* I.iii.22,
where Balurdo commends the words 'retort' and 'obtuse'. 'This trick of
playing with a new word, almost as if he wished to familiarise himself and
his audience with it, is typical of Marston' (Cross, *N. & Q.*, 200, 187):
cf. I Ant. & Mel., IV.ii.5–6.

          presently. I think Sir Geoffrey talks like a councillor.
          Go to, God's neaks, I think I tickle it.   [*Exit.*]

Pie. I'll seem to wind yon fool with kindest arm.   55
    He that's ambitious-minded, and but man,
    Must have his followers beasts, dubbed slavish sots
    Whose service is obedience and whose wit
    Reacheth no further than to admire their lord,
    And stare in adoration of his worth.   60
    I love a slave raked out of common mud
    Should seem to sit in counsel with my heart;
    High honoured blood's too squeamish to assent
    And lend a hand to an ignoble act;
    Poison from roses who could e'er abstract?   65

Enter PANDULPHO.

How now, Pandulpho, weeping for thy son?

SCENE II.

Pan. No, no, Piero, weeping for my sins;
    Had I been a good father he had been
    A gracious son.
Pie.   Pollution must be purged.
Pan. Why taint'st thou then the air with stench of flesh,
    And human putrifaction's noisome scent?   5
    I pray his body. Who less boon can crave

56. ambitious-minded] ambitious minded *Q*.   57. dubbed] *Q;* damn'd *Bullen.*   61. love] *Q;* loathe *Bullen.*   65.1.] *so Keltie; at II.ii.0.1 in Q.*
Scene 11] SCENA SECVNDA *Q; not in Keltie, Bullen, Hunter.*
2–3. Had ... been / A ... purged] *so Hunter;* Had ... sonne. / Pollution ... purg'd *Q.*

---

   54. *neaks*] a variant of 'nigs', a meaningless oath (*O.E.D.*, 'God' *sb.* 14 *b*).
   tickle it] ensure a satisfactory result (*O.E.D., vb.* 8).
   55. *wind*] embrace.
   57. *dubbed slavish sots*] i.e. slavish fools, knighted for their stupidity.
   65.]'who can turn a naturally good thing into evil' (Hunter).
   abstract]* to extract, or separate an essence (*O.E.D., vb.* 1. *c*).

Than to bestow upon the dead his grave?
Pie. Grave? Why? Think'st thou he deserves a grave
That hath defiled the temple of—
Pan.   Peace, peace!
Methinks I hear a humming murmur creep   10
From out his gellied wounds. Look on those lips,
Those now lawn pillows, on whose tender softness
Chaste modest speech, stealing from out his breast,
Had wont to rest itself, as loath to post
From out so fair an inn; look, look, they seem to stir   15
And breathe defiance to black obloquy.
Pie. Think'st thou thy son could suffer wrongfully?
Pan. A wise man wrongfully but never wrong
Can take; his breast's of such well-tempered proof
It may be rased, not pierced by savage tooth   20
Of foaming malice; showers of darts may dark
Heaven's ample brow, but not strike out a spark,

---

9. That . . . peace!] *so Hunter; two lines Q.*   19. well-tempered] well
tempered *Q.*

II.ii.10. *humming murmur*] Probably an allusion to the common belief
that the wounds of a victim of murder bled afresh in the presence of the
killer; *cf. R3*, I.ii.55–6, 'Dead Henry's wounds / Open their congeal'd
mouths and bleed afresh'.

11. *gellied*] congealed, coagulated.

12. *lawn*] A fine linen resembling cambric, here figurative for 'white' and
'soft', but Marston may also be alluding to the Italian practice of strangling
with a piece of lawn; *cf.* Marlowe, 'To strangle with a lawn thrust through
the throat' (Lightborn, *Edward II*, V.iv.32).

14. *post*] hasten.

16. *obloquy*] disgrace; *cf.* IV.iii.91.

18–19. *A wise . . . take*] A wise man may be subject to injustice, but can
never suffer injury from it.

19. *proof*] To be 'armed in proof' was to be invulnerable to attack, *cf.*
Bunyan, *Pilgrim's Progress* (Part I), 'they harnessed him [Christian] from
head to foot with what was of proof, lest perhaps he should meet with
assaults in the way' (ed. J. Thorpe, New York, 1969, p. 125).

20. *rased*] marked, scratched; 'the image is that of the foam-flecked
mouth of a savage animal' (Hunter).

21. *foaming*] Jonson condemns the figurative use of this word, *cf. Poet.*,
v.iii.287–8, '*bespawles / The conscious time, with humorous fome*': used twice
more by Marston in this play, II.iii.54 and III.v.18.

22. *strike out*] obliterate.

Much less pierce the sun's cheek. Such songs as these
I often dittied till my boy did sleep;
But now I turn plain fool; alas, I weep.   25
Pie. [*Aside*] 'Fore heaven he makes me shrug; would 'a
          were dead;
He is a virtuous man; what has our court to do
With virtue, in the devil's name! Pandulpho, hark:
My lustful daughter dies; start not, she dies.
I pursue justice, I love sanctity   30
And an undefiled temple of pure thoughts.
Shall I speak freely? Good Andrugio's dead;
And I do fear a fetch; but—umh! would I durst speak—
I do mistrust; but—umh! death! [*Aside*] Is he all, all man,
Hath he no part of mother in him, ha?   35
No lickerish womanish inquisitiveness?
Pan. Andrugio's dead!
Pie. Ay, and I fear his own unnatural blood,
To whom he gave life, hath given death for life.
[*Aside*] How could he come on! I see false suspect   40
Is viced, wrung hardly in a virtuous heart.
Well, I could give you reason for my doubts:
You are of honoured birth, my very friend;
You know how godlike 'tis to root out sin.
Antonio is a villain. Will you join   45
In oath with me against the traitor's life,
And swear you knew he sought his father's death?
I loved him well, yet I love justice more;
Our friends we should affect, justice adore.

24. I] *in some copies of Q the* I *has not printed.*   40. How] *Q;* Now *Hunter.*

---

26. *shrug*] i.e. with suppressed anger.
33. *fetch*] stratagem, trick: *cf.* Dekker, *Satiromastix*, IV.ii.121, 'Leave
your fetches and your fegaries'. Piero is preparing the way to blame Antonio
for the death of his father.
34. *all man*] i.e. composed entirely of masculine qualities.
36. *lickerish*] greedy, longing.
41. *viced*]* squeezed tightly (as in a vice), *O.E.D.,vb.*[1] 2.
49. *Our . . . affect*] we should love our friends; *cf.* I.ii.52.

Pan. My lord, the clapper of my mouth's not glibbed   50
    With court oil; 'twill not strike on both sides yet.

Pie. 'Tis just that subjects act commands of kings.

Pan. Command then just and honourable things.

Pie. Even so; myself then will traduce his guilt.

Pan. Beware, take heed, lest guiltless blood be spilt.   55

Pie. Where only honest deeds to kings are free
    It is no empire, but a beggary.

Pan. Where more than noble deeds to kings are free
    It is no empire, but a tyranny.

Pie. Tush, juiceless graybeard, 'tis immunity   60
    Proper to princes that our state exacts,
    Our subjects not alone to bear, but praise our acts.

Pan. O, but that prince that worthful praise aspires,
    From hearts, and not from lips, applause desires.

Pie. Pish! True praise the brow of common men doth ring,   65
    False only girts the temple of a king.
    He that hath strength and's ignorant of power,

---

50. *clapper*] tongue (of a bell); *cf. Ado*, III.ii.11, 'his tongue is the clapper'.

glibbed] made smooth (and thus insincere); *cf.* I.ii.17.

51. *on both sides*] i.e. I am not yet hypocrite enough to support both sides in controversy.

52–3.] *Cf.* Seneca, *Octavia*, 459–60: 'Nero. Iussisque nostris pareant. *Seneca.* Iusta impera— / *Nero.* Statuam ipse. *Seneca.* Quae consensus efficiat rata.' (*Nero.* Let them obey our orders. *Seneca.* Give righteous orders— *Nero.* I shall myself decide. *Seneca.* Which the general thought may ratify.)

54. *traduce*] blame, censure.

56–7.] *Cf.* Seneca, *Thyestes*, 214–15, 'Vbicumque tantum honesta dominanti licent, / precario regnatur.' (Where only right to a monarch is allowed, sovereignty is held on sufferance.)

57. *beggary*]* a place where beggars live (*O.E.D.*, 3).

60. *juiceless*]* withered.

60–63.] *Cf.* Seneca, *Thyestes*, 207–9, 'Maximum hoc regni bonum est, / quod facta domini cogitur populus sui / tam ferre quam laudare.' (The greatest advantage, this, of royal power, that their master's deeds the people are compelled as well to bear as praise).

65–6] *Cf.* Seneca, *Thyestes*, 211–12, 'Laus vera et humili saepe contingit viro, / non nisi potenti falsa.' (True praise even to the lowly often comes; false, only to the strong.)

66. *temple*] temples.

He was not made to rule, but to be ruled.
Pan. 'Tis praise to do, not what we can, but should.
Pie. Hence doting stoic! By my hope of bliss,   70
I'll make thee wretched.
Pan. Defiance to thy power, thou rifted jawn!
Now, by the loved heaven, sooner thou shalt
Rinse thy foul ribs from the black filth of sin
That soots thy heart, than make me wretched. Pish!   75
Thou canst not coop me up. Hadst thou a jail
With treble walls like antique Babylon,
Pandulpho can get out. I tell thee, Duke,
I have old Fortunatus' wishing-cap,
And can be where I list, even in a trice.   80
I'll skip from earth into the arms of heaven,
And from triumphal arch of blessedness
Spit on thy frothy breast. Thou canst not slave

79. wishing-cap] wishing cappe *Q*.

69.] *Cf.* Seneca, *Ocatvia*, 454, 'Id facere laus est quod decet, non quod licet.' ('Tis praiseworthy to do not what one may but what one ought.)

72. *rifted jawn*]* yawning abyss. Cotgrave defines 'To chawne, *se fendre gercer, crevasser, crever, se jarcer*'.

76. *coop*] imprison; *cf.* I.i.11 (used figuratively).

77. *treble . . . Babylon*] When Cyrus marched upon Babylon in 539 B.C. the city was fortified by first a Median Wall (which ran from near Opis on the Tigris to the outpost town of Sippar on the Euphrates); next a defensive wall just below the city (on the eastern bank of the Euphrates), and finally a third wall (on the river bank) forming a citadel around the temples, palaces and government offices.

79. *old Fortunatus*] In *Old Fortunatus*, by Thomas Dekker (1599), Fortunatus steals a magical hat from the Soldan of Babylon which, as the Soldan explains, 'clapt upon my head, / I (onely with a wish) am through the ayre, / Transported in a moment ouer Seas, / And ouer lands to any secrete place' (*Works*, ed. F. Bowers, I, II.i.86–9).

82. *triumphal arch*] Arches were used to welcome royalty on visits to cities, and speeches were often given by allegorical figures standing upon them; here it is an arch used to welcome the soul to heaven.

83. *frothy*] trifling, unsubstantial. Jonson ridicules the expression 'barmy froth' (vomited by Crispinus, *Poet.*, v.iii.492), and includes the phrase '*that puft-up lumpe of barmy froth*' (v.iii.284) in the poem he ascribes to Marston. Everard Guilpin uses the word in *Skialetheia* (1598), 'Let their sleight frothy minds be burbled up' (*sig.* E2).

Or banish me; I will be free at home,
Maugre the beard of greatness. The portholes   85
Of sheathèd spirit are ne'er corbed up,
But still stand open, ready to discharge
Their precious shot into the shrouds of heaven.
Pie. O torture! slave, I banish thee the town,
Thy native seat of birth.   90
Pan. How proud thou speak'st! I tell thee, Duke, the blasts
Of the swoll'n-cheekèd winds, nor all the breath of kings
Can puff me out my native seat of birth.
The earth's my body's, and the heaven's my soul's
Most native place of birth, which they will keep   95
Despite the menace of mortality.
Why, Duke,
That's not my native place where I was rocked:

86. corbed] *Q;* curb'd *Keltie, Hunter.*   92. swoll'n-cheeked] swolne
cheekt *Q.*

---

85. *maugre*] in spite of.
85–8. *The . . . heaven.*] A nautical metaphor to convey the idea of the
Stoic's superiority to misfortune. Pandulpho seems to be asserting that he
can always escape final catastrophe by suicide, which will send his soul to
heaven (released from the body like a charge from a cannon). The assertion
is presumably ironic, for, of course, suicide is not a passport to heaven.
portholes] Used figuratively (*O.E.D.,* 1. fig.), to express the ease by
which the soul may leave the body (through the mouth with the last
breath, or through a stab wound).
86. *sheathèd*] enclosed, protectively, by the body.
corbed]* closed, shut; this appears to be a coinage by Marston. W.
Huyshe (*Academy,* 36 (14 December 1889), 919, 388) suggests that it
is a nautical metaphor formed from either 'corbel' (Italian *corbello*) or
'corbeil' (French *corbeille*), meaning 'a basket filled with earth and used in
sieges'. Keltie and Hunter are assuming a spelling variant of 'curbed',
i.e. to check or rein in a horse.
88. *precious shot*] i.e. the soul.
shrouds] rigging.
89–99.] *Cf.* Whyttynton's *Seneca;* '*Sensualyte.* Thou shalt be banysshed.
Reason. My countre is nat forbyd me, but that place: into what lande so
ever I come I fynde it myne owne, there is no lande exyle, but a seconde
countre' (p. 45).
96. *menace of mortality*] threats of death.
98.] *Cf.* Whyttynton's *Seneca:* '*Reason.* My countre is in every place
where it is well, for that whiche is well, is in the man, nat in the place'
(p. 45).

A wise man's home is wheresoe'er he is wise.
Now, that from man, not from the place, doth rise.   100
Pie. Would I were deaf! O plague! Hence, dotard wretch.
Tread not in court. All that thou hast I seize.
[*Aside*] His quiet's firmer than I can disease.
Pan. Go, boast unto thy flatt'ring sycophants
Pandulpho's slave, Piero hath o'erthrown;   105
Loose fortune's rags are lost; my own's my own.

PIERO *going out, looks back.*

'Tis true, Piero, thy vexed heart shall see
Thou hast but tripped my slave, not conquered me.
Exeunt at several doors.

SCENE III.
Enter ANTONIO *with a book,* LUCIO, ALBERTO;
ANTONIO *in black.*

Alb. Nay, sweet, be comforted; take counsel and—
Ant. Alberto, peace! That grief is wanton-sick
Whose stomach can digest and brook the diet
Of stale ill-relished counsel. Pigmy cares

106.1. PIERO] *Bullen; Piero's Q.*   108.1.] *so Bullen; after l. 106.1 in Q.*
Scene III] SCENA TERTIA *Q;* SCENE II *Keltie, Bullen, Hunter.*
2. wanton-sick] wanton sick *Q.*   4. ill-relished] ill relisht *Q.*

---

100. *that*] i.e. wisdom.
103. *disease*] infect with disturbance.
105. *Pandulpho's . . . o'erthrown*] i.e. that Piero has overcome the physical and temporal in Pandulpho and reduced him to the condition of slavery.
106. *my . . . own*] I am still self-sufficient.
108. *tripped my slave*] i.e. merely made my physical body (the slave of my soul) stumble.

II.iii. 0.1.] *Cf. Ham.,* II.ii.166.1, '*Enter* HAMLET, *reading on a book*'; and cf. *Spanish Tragedy*, III.xiii.0.1, '*Enter* HIERONIMO *with a book in his hand*' (this is a volume of Seneca, as is Antonio's book).
2. *wanton-sick*] excessively sick.
4. *ill-relished*] tasteless.
4–6.] *Cf.* Seneca, *Medea,* 155–6, 'Levis est dolor qui capere consilium potest / et clepere sese; magna non latitant mala.' (Light is the grief which can take counsel and hide itself; great ills lie not in hiding.)

Can shelter under patience' shield, but giant griefs   5
Will burst all covert.

Luc.   My lord, 'tis supper time.

Ant. Drink deep, Alberto; eat, good Lucio;
But my pined heart shall eat on naught but woe.

Alb. My lord, we dare not leave you thus alone.

Ant. You cannot leave Antonio alone.   10
The chamber of my breast is even thronged
With firm attendance that forswears to flinch.
I have a thing sits here; it is not grief,
'Tis not despair, nor the most plague
That the most wretched are infected with;   15
But the most grief-full, despairing, wretched,
Accursed, miserable—O, for heaven's sake
Forsake me now; you see how light I am,
And yet you force me to defame my patience.

Luc. Fair gentle prince—   20

Ant. Away! thy voice is hateful; thou dost buzz,
And beat my ears with intimations
That Mellida, that Mellida is light
And stainèd with adulterous luxury.
I cannot brook't. I tell thee, Lucio,   25
Sooner will I give faith that virtue's cant
In princes' courts will be adorned with wreath

---

6. Will . . . time.] *so Hunter; two lines Q.*   16. grief-full] *1633;* greefull *Q.*
26. cant] *Bullen;* scant *Q.*

---

6. *burst all covert*] i.e. force their way, like game from shelter (of a thicket).
14. *most*] greatest.
18. *light*] volatile, unstable.
19. *defame*] to repudiate and thus dishonour.
23. *light*] unchaste.
24. *adulterous luxury*] wanton lechery.
26. *cant*] 'the corner or niche in which the statue of Virtue was placed' (Bullen); *cf.* Middleton, *Part of the Entertainment to King James, Works,* ed. Bullen, VII.222, 'Directly under her, in a cant by herself, was ARETE (Virtue), enthroned'. Hunter points out that the term is also being used figuratively to mean 'empty professions'.

Of choice respect, and endeared intimate;
Sooner will I believe that friendship's rein
Will curb ambition from utility,   30
Than Mellida is light. Alas, poor soul,
Didst e'er see her, good heart, hast heard her speak?
Kind, kind soul. Incredulity itself
Would not be so brass-hearted as suspect
So modest cheeks.

Luc.   My lord—

Ant.   Away!   35
A self-one guilt doth only hatch distrust;
But a chaste thought's as far from doubt, as lust.
I entreat you, leave me.

Alb. Will you endeavour to forget your grief?

Ant. I'faith I will, good friend, i'faith I will.   40
I'll come and eat with you. Alberto, see
I am taking physic, here's philosophy.   [*Shows book.*]
Good honest, leave me; I'll drink wine anon.

Alb. Since you enforce us, fair prince, we are gone.

                         Exeunt ALBERTO *and* LUCIO.

                ANTONIO *reads*:

Ferte fortiter: hoc est quo deum antecedatis. Ille enim   45
extra patientiam malorum; vos supra. Contemnite dolorem:

---

34. brass-hearted] brasse hearted *Q*.   34–6. Would . . . suspect / So . . .
Away! / A . . . distrust] *so this ed.;* Would . . . cheeks / My Lord / Away . . .
distrust *Q*.   36. self-one] *Q;* self-sown *Bullen.*

---

28. *endeared intimate*] The phrase appears to be used seriously here to
mean 'loved like a close friend', but *cf.* II.i.48; 'ate' is a favourite Marstonian
suffix; see I.i.103 n.
    30. *from utility*] from being used.
    36. *self-one*]* (?) alone with itself (*O.E.D.*, 'self' 3. *a*); this seems to be a
coinage by Marston. The meaning of the line appears to be 'a mind
isolated by its own guilt instinctively suspects other people's motives'.
    37. *as lust*] i.e. as it is from lust.
    42. Shows book] i.e. a volume of Seneca.
    45–8.] From Seneca, *De Providentia*, VI.6, 'ferte fortiter. Hoc est quo
deum antecedatis; ille extra patientiam malorum est, vos supra patientiam
. . . Contemnite dolorem; aut solvetur aut solvet . . . Contemnite fortunam;

aut solvetur, aut solvet. Contemnite fortunam: nullum
telum, quo feriret animum habet.

Pish! Thy mother was not lately widowed,
Thy dear affièd love lately defamed   50
With blemish of foul lust when thou wrotest thus.
Thou, wrapped in furs, beaking thy limbs 'fore fires
Forbid'st the frozen zone to shudder. Ha, ha! 'tis naught
But foamy bubbling of a fleamy brain,
Naught else but smoke. O, what dank, marish spirit   55
But would be fired with impatience
At my—
No more, no more; he that was never blest
With height of birth, fair expectation
Of mounted fortunes, knows not what it is   60
To be the pitied object of the world.
O poor Antonio, thou mayst sigh!

Mel. [*Within*] Ay me!
Ant.   And curse—

47–8. *fortunam: nullen telum*] *Q; fortunas: nullus telus Halliwell; fortunas;*
nullus telum Keltie.   57–8. At my— / No ... blest] *so Bullen; one line Q.*
63. *Mel.* [*Within*] *Hunter; Mel.* [*from beneath*] *Bullen.*

---

nullum illi telum quo feriret animum dedi.' (. . . endure with fortitude. In
this you may outstrip God; he is exempt from enduring evil, while you are
superior to it . . . Scorn pain; it will either be relieved or relieve you . . .
Scorn Fortune; I have given her no weapon with which she may strike
your soul.) Marston's substitution of 'habet' for 'dedi' modifies the last
phrase by making it impersonal, i.e. 'Scorn Fortune; it has no weapon
with which to strike your soul'.

50. *affièd*] betrothed.
51. *wrotest*] This is a monosyllable.
52–3.] i.e. Protected from exposure (to the elements and danger) yourself, you try to prevent other people responding normally to exposure.
    beaking] warming (*O.E.D.*, 'beek' v.¹ 1).
54. *foamy . . . brain*] the superficial emptiness of a detached phlegmatic
temperament. Jonson condemns the figurative use of *foamy*, see II.ii.21 n.
    bubbling]★ *O.E.D.*, vb.¹ sb. 1. *fig.*; cf. *What You Will*, Wood, II.232,
'what a leaprous humor / Breaks from ranke swelling of these bubbling
wits ?'
    fleamy] A variant of 'phlegmy' or 'phlegmatic'; Cf. *Fawn*, IV.i.199,
'fleamy loathsomeness'.
55. *marish*] marsh-like.

Pan. [*Within*]   Black powers.

Ant.   And cry—

Mar. [*Within*]   O heaven!

Ant. And close laments with—

Alb. [*Within*]   O me, most miserable!

Pan. [*Within*] Woe for my dear, dear son!   65

Mar. [*Within*] Woe for my dear, dear husband!

Mel. [*Within*] Woe for my dear, dear love.

Ant. Woe for me all; close all your woes in me,
    In me, Antonio. Ha! Where live these sounds?
    I can see nothing; grief's invisible   70
    And lurks in secret angles of the heart.
    Come, sigh again, Antonio bears his part.

Mel. [*Behind the grating.*]
    O here, here is a vent to pass my sighs.
    I have surcharged the dungeon with my plaints;
    Prison and heart will burst if void of vent.   75
    Ay, that is Phoebe, empress of the night,
    That 'gins to mount. O chastest deity,
    If I be false to my Antonio,
    If the least soil of lust smears my pure love,
    Make me more wretched, make me more accursed   80
    Than infamy, torture, death, hell, and heaven

63–4. Ay . . . heaven! / And . . . miserable!] *so Hunter; each phrase a separate line in Q.*   64. S.H. *Alb.*] *Q; Mel.* [*from beneath*] *Bullen.* 72.1.] *This ed.;* [*speaks through the grating*] *Hunter.*

65–8. *Cf. Spanish Tragedy*, III.vii.61–3, 'Woe to the cause of these constrained wars, / Woe to thy baseness and captivity, / Woe to thy birth, thy body and thy soul'.

68. *close*] bring to a 'full close' (as in music); *cf.* Dryden 'A Song for St Cecilia's Day' (1687), 'From Harmony, from heav'nly Harmony / This universal Frame began: / From Harmony to Harmony / Through all the compass of the Notes it ran, / The Diapason closing full in Man' (ll. 10–14).

72. *bears his part*] i.e. sings his part of the music.

74. *surcharged*] overburdened, overloaded; *cf. Spanish Tragedy*, III.vii.3–4, 'mine exclaims, that have surcharg'd the air / With ceaseless plaints'.

76. *Phoebe*] i.e. Artemis, as goddess of the moon; the moon.

Can bound with amplest power of thought; if not,
Purge my poor heart from defamation's blot.
Ant. 'Purge my poor heart from defamation's blot'!
Poor heart, how like her virtuous self she speaks.   85
Mellida, dear Mellida, it is Antonio;
Slink not away, 'tis thy Antonio.
Mel. How found you out, my lord? Alas, I know
'Tis easy in this age to find out woe.
I have a suit to you.
Ant.   What is't, dear soul?   90
Mel. Kill me. I'faith, I'll wink, not stir a jot.
For God sake, kill me. In sooth, loved youth,
I am much injured, look, see how I creep.
I cannot wreak my wrong, but sigh and weep.
Ant. May I be cursèd, but I credit thee.   95
Mel. Tomorrow I must die.
Ant.   Alas, for what?
Mel. For loving thee. 'Tis true, my sweetest breast,
I must die falsely; so must thou, dear heart.
Nets are a-knitting to entrap thy life.
Thy father's death must make a paradise   100
To my (I shame to call him) father. Tell me, sweet,
Shall I die thine? Dost love me still, and still?
Ant. I do.
Mel.   Then welcome heaven's will.
Ant.   Madam,

83. from] *1633;* with *Q.*   90. I . . . soul] *so Hunter; two lines Q.*   96.
Tomorrow . . . what?] *so Hunter; two lines Q.*   99. a-knitting] a knitting *Q.*
103–4. I . . . Madam / I . . . tragedian] *so Hunter;* I doe / Then . . . will. /
Madam . . . in for- *Q.*

---

82. *bound . . . thought*] i.e. encompass with the most extreme reach of the
human imagination.
83. *defamation's blot*] the smear of slander.
91. *wink*] shut my eyes.
94. *wreak*] avenge; cf. *Rom.*, III.v.101–2, 'To wreak the love I bore my
cousin Tybalt / Upon his body'.
102. *still*] for ever.

I will not swell like a tragedian
In forcèd passion of affected strains.   105
If I had present power of ought but pitying you
I would be as ready to redress your wrongs
As to pursue your love. Throngs of thoughts
Crowd for their passage; somewhat I will do.
Reach me thy hand; think this is honour's bent   110
To live unslaved, to die innocent.

Mel. Let me entreat a favour, gracious love:
Be patient, see me die; good, do not weep;
Go sup, sweet chuck, drink and securely sleep.

Ant. I'faith I cannot, but I'll force my face   115
To palliate my sickness.

Mel. Give me thy hand. Peace on thy bosom dwell;
That's all my woe can breathe; kiss, thus farewell.

Ant. Farewell. My heart is great of thoughts—stay dove—
And therefore I must speak. But what, O love?   120
By this white hand, no more! Read in these tears
What crushing anguish thy Antonio bears.

ANTONIO *kisseth* MELLIDA'S *hand; then* MELLIDA
goes from the grate.

Mel. Good night, good heart.
Ant. Thus heat from blood, thus souls from bodies part.

Enter PIERO *and* STROTZO.

Pie. He grieves; laugh, Strotzo, laugh; he weeps.   125
Hath he tears? O pleasure! Hath he tears?
Now do I scourge Andrugio with steel whips

105–9.] *so 1633; prose in* Q.   119.] *so Hunter; two lines in* Q.   121. hand,
no] *1633;* hand: eno Q.   123. Good] *1633;* God Q.

---

104. *swell*] i.e. take up a pose.
105. *affected strains*] assumed tones, adopted with an effort.
110. *bent*] inclination.
115–6. *but . . . sickness*] but I will compel my face to disguise my true
feelings.
119. *great of*]* pregnant with (*O.E.D., adj.* 3. *b. fig*).

Of knotty vengeance. Strotzo, cause me straight
Some plaining ditty to augment despair.   [*Exit* STROTZO.]
Triumph, Piero; hark, he groans, O rare!   130
Ant.   Behold a prostrate wretch laid on his tomb;
His epitaph thus: *Ne plus ultra*. Ho!
Let none out-woe me, mine's Herculean woe.

They sing.

Exit PIERO *at the end of the song.*

SCENE IV.
Enter MARIA.

Ant.   May I be more cursed than heaven
Can make me if I am not more wretched
Than man can conceive me. Sore forlorn orphan,
What omnipotence can make thee happy?
Mar.   How now, sweet son; good youth, what dost thou?   5
Ant.   Weep, weep.

---

129. S.D.] *Bullen; not in Keltie, who directs* [STROTZO *sings*] *after l. 133.*
133. *They sing*] *This ed.;* CANTANT *Q; A song within Bullen.*
Scene IV] SCENA QVARTA *Q; not in Keltie, Bullen, Hunter.*
1–4.] *so Hunter;* May . . . me / If . . . wretched / Then . . . forlorne /
Orphant . . . happie *Q;* May . . . if / I'm . . . me. / Sore . . . omnipotence /
Can . . . happy? *Bullen.*   5. How . . . thou?] *so Hunter;* How . . . youth,
/ what . . . thou? *Q.*   6. Weep . . . weep.] *so this ed.; two lines Q.*

---

128. *knotty*] i.e. of the knots in a whip, and of the difficulties in the way
of revenge.
129. *plaining ditty*] pathetic song.
131. *his tomb*] the earth.
132. *Ne plus ultra*] Nothing beyond. The motto alleged to have been
inscribed upon the Pillars of Hercules.
133. *Herculean woe*] Probably an allusion to the death of Hercules,
caused by a poison from the centaur Nessus spread on his tunic by
Deineira, in the mistaken belief that it was a love charm, to win her
husband back from his new concubine, Iole. The poison on the tunic
eroded the skin.
133.1.] Piero sends Strotzo to arrange a 'plaining ditty' to conclude this
scene (see ll. 128–9 above), and Piero and Antonio can hardly be the
singers, for it is designed to deepen Antonio's grief: presumably it is sung
by the choirboys in the gallery.

Mar.   Dost naught but weep, weep?
Ant. Yes, mother, I do sigh and wring my hands,
         Beat my poor breast and wreathe my tender arms.
         Hark ye, I'll tell you wondrous strange, strange news.
Mar. What my good boy, stark mad?
Ant.   I am not.   10
Mar. Alas, is that strange news?
Ant. 'Strange news'—why mother, is't not wondrous strange
         I am not mad, I run not frantic, ha?
         Knowing my father's trunk scarce cold, your love
         Is sought by him that doth pursue my life;   15
         Seeing the beauty of creation,
         Antonio's bride, pure heart, defamed and stowed
         Under the hatches of obscuring earth.
         Heu quo labor, quo vota ceciderunt mea?

                    Enter PIERO.

Pie. Good evening to the fair Antonio,   20
         Most happy fortune, sweet succeeding time,
         Rich hope; think not thy fate a bankrout though—
Ant. [*Aside*] Umh, the devil in his good time and tide for-
         sake thee!
Pie. How now? hark ye, prince.
Ant.   God be with you.
Pie. Nay, noble blood, I hope ye not suspect—   25
Ant. 'Suspect'? I scorn't. Here's cap and leg, good night.
         [*Aside*] Thou that wants power, with dissemblance fight.

10. What . . . not.] *so this ed.; two lines Q.*   24. How . . . you] *so this ed.;*
two lines Q.

II.iv. 10. *mad*] *Cf. Ham.*, II.i, where Hamlet is assumed by Polonius to be
mad with love for Ophelia.
     18. *Under the hatches*] under the decks.
     19.] Seneca, *Octavia*, 632, 'Alas! to what end my labour and my
prayers?'
     22. *bankrout*] bankrupt.
     26. *cap and leg*] i.e. I uncover my head and bow to you (with the
suggestion of courtly duplicity).

Exit ANTONIO.

Pie. Madam, O that you could remember to forget.
Mar. I had a husband and a happy son.
Pie. Most powerful beauty, that enchanting grace—   30
Mar. Talk not of beauty nor enchanting grace:
    My husband's dead, my son's distraught, accursed.
    Come, I must vent my griefs, or heart will burst.

Exit MARIA.

Pie. She's gone, and yet she's here; she hath left a print
    Of her sweet graces fixed within my heart   35
    As fresh as is her face. I'll marry her.
    She's most fair, true; most chaste, most false;
    Because most fair, 'tis firm I'll marry her.

Scene v.
Enter STROTZO

Str. My lord.
Pie. Ha, Strotzo, my other soul, my life.
    Dear, hast thou steeled the point of thy resolve?
    Will't not turn edge in execution?
Str. No.   5
Pie. Do it with rare passion, and present thy guilt.
    As if 'twere wrung out with thy conscience gripe.
    Swear that my daughter's innocent of lust
    And that Antonio bribed thee to defame
    Her maiden honour, on inveterate hate   10

---

37. fair . . . false;] *Punctuation this ed.;* fair, true, most chaste, most false:
Q; fair, —true; most chaste, —false; *Bullen;* fair—true! most chaste—
most false! *Hunter.*

Scene v] SCENA QVINTA *Q; not in Keltie, Bullen, Hunter.*

28–33.] Imitated from the wooing of Anne by Richard of Gloucester,
R3, I.ii.33 ff.
    37. *most false*] Because she is Andrugio's widow.
    II.v. 7. *with . . . gripe*] i.e. through the distress caused by conscience;
cf. III.iii.19.

Unto my blood; and that thy hand was fee'd
By his large bounty for his father's death.
Swear plainly that thou chokedst Andrugio,
By his son's only egging. Rush me in
Whilst Mellida prepares herself to die,   15
Halter about thy neck, and with such sighs,
Laments and acclamations lifen it,
As if impulsive power of remorse—

Str. I'll weep.

Pie. Ay, ay, fall on thy face and cry, 'Why suffer you   20
So lewd a slave as Strotzo is to breathe?'

Str. I'll beg a strangling, grow importunate—

Pie. As if thy life were loathsome to thee; then I
Catch straight the cord's end, and, as much incensed
With thy damned mischiefs, offer a rude hand   25
As ready to gird in thy pipe of breath;
But on the sudden straight I'll stand amazed,
And fall in exclamations of thy virtues.

Str. Applaud my agonies and penitence.

Pie. Thy honest stomach that could not digest   30
The crudities of murder; but, surcharged,
Vomited'st them up in Christian piety.

Str. Then clip me in your arms,

Pie. And call thee brother, mount thee straight to state,
Make thee of council; tut, tut, what not, what not?   35

17. lifen] *Q;* liven *Keltie et al.*

---

14. *Rush me in*] i.e. rush in to me.
17. *acclamations*] outcries.
lifen]* make lifelike; *cf.* Webster, *The White Devil*, 'To the Reader',
18–19, 'enrich it with the sententious *Chorus*, and as it were lifen death'.
18. *impulsive*]* determining (to action) (*O.E.D.,a.* 2.[*fig.*]).
22. *importunate*]* persistently troublesome (*O.E.D.,a.* 2. *b*).
26. *to gird . . . breath*] i.e. to strangle you; Jonson appears to condemn
'gird' used figuratively, *Poet.*,v.iii.382, 'you shall eternally girt me to you'.
31. *crudities*]* undigested (and undigestible) pieces of food, or im-
perfectly 'concocted' humours; here figurative for 'moral revulsion'
(*O.E.D.*,2.*fig.*).
34. *state*] i.e. promote you to my council of state.

Think on't, be confident, pursue the plot.

Str.   Look, here's a troop: 'a true rogue's lips are mute.'
I do not use to speak, but execute.
He lays finger on his mouth, and draws his dagger.   [*Exit.*]

Pie.   So, so; run headlong to confusion,
Thou slight-brained mischief; thou art made as dirt   40
To plaster up the bracks of my defects.
I'll wring what may be squeezed from out his use,
And good night, Strotzo. Swell plump, bold heart,
For now thy tide of vengeance rolleth in.
O now *Tragoedia Cothurnata* mounts;   45
Piero's thoughts are fixed on dire exploits;
Pell mell! Confusion and black murder guides
The organs of my spirit—shrink not, heart;
Capienda rebus in malis praeceps via est.

[*Exit.*]

The end of the Second Act.

40. slight-brained] slight brain'd *Q.*   49.2.] *This ed.;* FINIS ACTVS
SECVNDI. *Q.*

---

37. *troop*] a trope, a figurative way of speaking.
40. *slight-brained*] dull-witted.
41. *bracks*] cracks, ruptures; *cf. I Ant. & Mel.*, Ind., 55–6, 'to stitch up
the bracks of unworthily honor'd'.
45. Tragoedia Cothurnata] The *Kothurnoi* on the Greek stage were the
thick-soled boots (or buskins) worn by the actors; the origin of this phrase
is Ovid, *Tristia*, II.553–4, 'et dedimus tragicis scriptum regale cothurnis, /
quaeque gravis debet verba cothurnus habet', which Thomas Heywood
translates (*Apology for Actors*, 1612, *sig.* D2) 'With royall stile speakes our
Cothurnate Muse, / A buskind phrase in buskin'd playes we use.' Here the
immediate derivation is from *The Spanish Tragedy*, IV.i.159–61, 'Give me a
stately-written Tragedy, / *Tragedia cothurnata*, fitting kings, / Containing
matter, and not common things.' On the grounds that this tragic mode is
old-fashioned Jonson seems to sneer at this phrase in *Poet.*, v.iii.280–2,
'*Alas! That were no moderne consequence, / To have corthurnall buskins
frighted hence*'. These lines are included in the poem ascribed to Crispinus
(Marston).
49.] A variant of Seneca, *Agamemnon*, 154, 'Rapienda rebus in malis
praeceps via est'. (In the midst of ills, we must snatch at headlong ways.)
The substitution of *Capienda* moderates the meaning to 'In the midst of
ills, we must take hold of the steepest path'.

Act III

SCENE I.

A dumb show. The cornets sounding for the Act.

Enter CASTILIO *and* FOROBOSCO, ALBERTO *and* BALURDO *with poleaxes;* STROTZO *talking with* PIERO; [PIERO] *seemeth to send out* STROTZO; *exit* STROTZO. *Enter* STROTZO, MARIA, NUTRICHE *and* LUCIO. PIERO *passeth through his guard and talks with* MARIA *with seeming amorousness; she seemeth to reject his suit, flies to the tomb, kneels and kisseth it.* PIERO *bribes* NUTRICHE *and* LUCIO; *they go to her, seeming to solicit his suit. She riseth, offers to go out;* PIERO *stayeth her, tears open his breast, embraceth and kisseth her; and so they go all out in state.*

Enter two Pages, the one with two tapers, the other with a chafing-dish; a perfume in it. ANTONIO, *in his nightgown and a nightcap, unbraced, following after.*

Ant. The black jades of swart night trot foggy rings
　　　'Bout heaven's brow. 　　　　　　　[*Clock strikes twelve.*]
　　　　　　　　　'Tis now stark dead night.
　　Is this Saint Mark's Church?
1st. Page. It is, my lord.
Ant. 　　　　　　　　Where stands my father's hearse?

11.i.0.5. MARIA] *Bullen; her Q.*　　0.11. *Enter*] *Q; After the dumb show, enter Bullen.*　　2. *Clock strikes twelve.*] *Bullen;* (12) *Q.*　　4. It . . . hearse?] *so this ed.; two lines Q.*

___

　　III. This act takes place 'within', during the hours of darkness; scenes i–iii occur in the church and iv and v in Maria's bedchamber.
　　0.3. poleaxes] halberds.
　　0.11–12. chafing-dish] a portable grate (acting as a censer).
　　1. *swart*] dark, swarthy; *cf.* III.ii.25.
　　　　jades] worn-out old horses; *cf.* I.v.72.
　　2. *stark dead night*] the absolute point of intensest darkness; *cf.* I.i.3 n.

2nd. *Page* Those streamers bear his arms. Ay, that is it.   5
Ant. Set tapers to the tomb and lamp the church;
    Give me the fire. Now depart and sleep.   *Exeunt Pages.*
    I purify the air with odorous fume. [*Swings the chafing-dish.*]
    Graves, vaults, and tombs, groan not to bear my weight,
    Cold flesh, bleak trunks, wrapped in your half-rot
      shrouds,   10
    I press you softly with a tender foot.
    Most honoured sepulchre, vouchsafe a wretch
    Leave to weep o'er thee. Tomb, I'll not be long
    Ere I creep in thee, and with bloodless lips
    Kiss my cold father's cheek. I pray thee, grave,   15
    Provide soft mould to wrap my carcass in.
    Thou royal spirit of Andrugio,
    Where'er thou hover'st, airy intellect,
    I heave up tapers to thee—view thy son—
    In celebration of due obsequies.   20
    Once every night I'll dew thy funeral hearse
    With my religious tears.
    O, blessèd father of a cursèd son,
    Thou died'st most happy since thou lived'st not
    To see thy son most wretched and thy wife   25
    Pursued by him that seeks my guiltless blood.

8. *Swings the chafing-dish.*] *Hunter subst.*   15. pray thee] *Hunter;* pree thee *Q;* prithee *Bullen.*   17–19. Thou . . . Andrugio, / Where'er . . . intellect, / I . . . son] *so Bullen;* Thou . . . hoverest / Ayrie . . . son *Q.*

---

5. *streamers . . . arms*] Narrow, pointed flags or pennons which bear his coat of arms (probably standing upright behind or beside the hearse).
6. *lamp*] light up (by hanging lamps).
7. *fire*] i.e. the chafing-dish, which he proceeds to swing, using it as a censer.
8. *fume*] i.e. sweet-smelling smoke; *cf.* I.v.89.
10. *half-rot*] i.e. half rotten; *cf.* 'half rot searcloaths', *Sophonisba* (Wood, II.46).
18. *intellect*]* spirit, intelligence (*O.E.D.*, sb. 2. *transf.*).
19. *heave up*] raise, in the sense of 'exalt'.
20. *obsequies*] funeral rites.
23.] Hunter compares *Spanish Tragedy*, IV.iv.84 ff, where Hieronimo laments his misery while showing the body of his dead son.

O, in what orb thy mighty spirit soars,
Stoop and beat down this rising fog of shame
That strives to blur thy blood and girt defame
About my innocent and spotless brows.   30
Non est mori miserum, sed misere mori.

[*Enter Ghost.*]

Ghost of And. Thy pangs of anguish rip my cerecloth up;
And lo, the ghost of old Andrugio
Forsakes his coffin! Antonio, revenge!
I was empoisoned by Piero's hand;   35
Revenge my blood!—take spirit, gentle boy—
Revenge my blood! Thy Mellida is chaste;
Only to frustrate thy pursuit in love
Is blazed unchaste. Thy mother yields consent
To be his wife and give his blood a son,   40
That made her husbandless and doth complot
To make her sonless. But before I touch
The banks of rest, my ghost shall visit her.
Thou vigour of my youth, juice of my love,
Seize on revenge, grasp the stern-bended front   45

32. S.H.] *Bullen; And. Q.*   45. stern-bended] sterne bended *Q.*

---

27. *what*] whatever.

29. *girt*] fasten, tie; a now rare spelling of 'gird'.

31.] 'It is not a wretched thing to die, but it is to die wretchedly' (trans. Keltie). The source of this tag remains unidentified.

32. *cerecloth*] winding sheet.

35. *I . . . hand*] Cf. the Ghost's revelation to Hamlet, I.v.38–40, 'know, thou noble youth, / The serpent that did sting thy father's life / Now wears his crown'.

39. *blazed*] proclaimed abroad.

45. *stern-bended front*] frowning forehead.

45–6. *Seize . . . clutch*] This emblematic concept of the figure of Vengeance is represented with a bent-down forehead, prominent enough to be seized by the avenger. Earlier Marston describes this figure as having 'curled snaky locks' (II.i.7–8) and, perhaps, carring a knotted steel whip (II.iii.127–8). Vengeance is a violent man, normally caged (see I.i.11–12 n.), who sucks blood (III.iii.35–6) and accepts blood as incense (III.iii.62); he towers up, clutching his fist, ready to bring it down to crush the guilty

Of frowning vengeance with unpeisèd clutch.
Alarum Nemesis, rouse up thy blood,
Invent some stratagem of vengeance
Which, but to think on, may like lightning glide
With horror through thy breast. Remember this: 50
Scelera non ulcisceris, nisi vincis.

                                    Exit ANDRUGIO'S *ghost.*

SCENE II.

Enter MARIA, *her hair about her ears,*
NUTRICHE *and* LUCIO *with Pages and torches.*

Mar. Where left you him ? Show me, good boys. Away!

                                    [*Exeunt Pages.*]

46. unpeisèd] *This ed.;* vnpaized *Q;* impeised *Hunter.*

Scene II] SCENA SECVNDA *Q; not in Keltie, Bullen, Hunter.*

(v.i.3–6); also, perhaps, he foams at the lips with blood (III.v.17–18). When
thwarted, however, he is bent beneath the oppression of the need for
fulfilment (III.v.11). I have been unable to discover any emblematic tradition from which this figure could be derived (unlike the figure of Opportunity, v.iii.59 n.). Marston's picture of Vengeance probably originates with
him.

46. *unpeisèd*]* Marston uses the word 'peise' elsewhere in both simple
(Prol. 29 and n., and v.i.5) and compound forms (I.v.97): he consistently
spells it 'pais[or z]e'. The Q reading here, 'vnpaized', is unusual, but
Marston made a habit of the unusual in vocabulary, and the compositor is
unlikely to have modified the more common 'impaized' to the unique
'unpaized'. Hunter's emendation ('impeised', glossed as 'weighty') is therefore unconvincing. The image created in ll. 45–6 (see note above) is of an
avenger clutching the bent brow of Vengeance, and later, at v.i.3–6,
Marston describes Vengeance as towering aloft with a bunched fist ready
to crush the guilty—this latter situation is presumably the result of
Antonio's unwavering resolution. An 'unpeisèd clutch' is therefore one
which is so resolute that it is not weighed down by the severity of the task,
and is thus able to lift up the bent brow of Vengeance so that it may
'tower aloft'.

47. *Alarum Nemesis*] awake Vengeance.

51.] Seneca, *Thyestes,* 195–6, 'You do not avenge crimes unless you
conquer' (trans. Keltie).

III.ii.0.1. hair about her ears] a symptom of distraction, or grief.

Nut. God's me, your hair!

Mar.   Nurse, 'tis not yet proud day;
       The neat gay mistress of the light's not up,
       Her cheeks not yet slurred over with the paint
       Of borrowed crimson; the unprankèd world   5
       Wears yet the night-clothes. Let flare my loosed hair;
       I scorn the presence of the night.
       Where's my boy? Run! I'll range about the church
       Like frantic Bacchanal or Jason's wife
       Invoking all the spirits of the graves   10
       To tell me where. Ha! O, my poor wretched blood,
       What dost thou up at midnight, my kind boy?
       Dear soul, to bed. O, thou hast struck a fright
       Unto thy mother's panting—

Ant.   *O quisquis nova*   15
       Supplicia functis durus umbrarum arbiter
       Disponis, quisquis exeso iaces

---

2. God's ... day] *so Hunter; two lines Q.*   3. mistress] *Wood (conj. Daniel);*
mistes *Q.*   15. S.H.] *Bullen; not in Q.*   16. durus] *Hunter; dirus Q.*

---

2. *Gods' me*] i.e. God save me.
   proud] splendid, magnificent (in the sense of 'full').
3. *neat*] trim, elegant; possibly parodied by Jonson, *Poet.*, III.i.30, 'By
PHOEBVS, here's a most neate fine street.'
   mistress of the light] Aurora.
4. *slurred*]* smeared, stained (*O.E.D.*, *vb.*[1] 1).
5. *unprankèd*]* not yet dressed.
6. *flare*] stream in the wind.
7. *presence*] ceremonial chamber.
8. *range*] roam.
9.] i.e. like Agave (in Euripides' *Bacchae*) or Medea.
15–22.] Seneca, *Thyestes*, 'O quisquis ... Disponis', ll. 13–15; 'quisquis ...
horres', ll. 75–9; *Antonii* ... *vos*, ll. 80–1. The words '*Antonii*' and
'*Ulciscar*' are Marston's own, otherwise the Latin text, as here emended,
corresponds with both the seventeenth-century and modern versions of
Seneca's text. 'O whoe'er thou art, harsh judge of shades, who dost allot
fresh punishments to the dead ... whoe'er liest quaking beneath the
hollowed rock, and fearest the downfall of the mountainous mass even now
coming on thee; who'er shudderest at the fierce gaping of greedy lions,
and, entangled in their toils, dost shudder at the dread ranks of furies; ...
hear ye the words of Antonio now hastening to you: "I shall revenge".'

Pavidus sub antro, quisquis venturi times
Montis ruinam, quisquis avidorum feros,
Rictus leonum, et dira furiarum agmina   20
Implicitus horres, Antonii vocem excipe
Properantis ad vos: Ulciscar.

Mar. Alas, my son's distraught. Sweet boy, appease
      Thy mutining affections.

Ant. By the astoning terror of swart night,   25
      By the infectious damps of clammy graves,
      And by the mould that presseth down
      My dead father's skull, I'll be revenged!

Mar. Wherefore? on whom? for what? Go, go to bed,
      Good, duteous son. Ho, but thy idle—   30

Ant. So I may sleep, tombed in an honoured hearse,
      So may my bones rest in that sepulchre.

Mar. Forget not duty, son; to bed, to bed.

Ant. May I be cursèd by my father's ghost
      And blasted with incensèd breath of heaven   35
      If my heart beat on ought but vengeance.
      May I be numbed with horror and my veins
      Pucker with singeing torture, if my brain
      Digest a thought but of dire vengeance;
      May I be fettered slave to coward chance,   40

---

18. *antro*] *1633; antri Q.*   19. *feros*] *Bullen; feres Q.*   20. *et*] *Halliwell;*
& Q.   24. *mutining*] *Q; mutinous Halliwell, Keltie, Wood.*

23–4. *appease . . . affections*] 'set your disturbed mind at rest' (Hunter).

25. *astoning*]* stunning, paralysing (*O.E.D., ppl. a. a*).

30. *idle*] foolish.

36. *beat*]* Bullen compares *Tempest,* v.i.246–7, 'Do not infest your mind
with beating on / The strangeness of this business'; and Cross (*N. & Q.,*
202, 525.) points out that Marston conflates the senses of *beat vb.*[1] 9 *intr.,*
'to insist with iteration *on* or *upon*', and 13. *intr.,* 'to throb, pulsate (of the
heart)'. Thus he creates a new sense not in *O.E.D.*

36, 39, 41. *vengeance*] a trisyllable: mocked by Jonson, *Poet.,* v.iii.293,
'*Of strenuous venge-ance to clutch the fist*'; used again by Marston as a
trisyllable in *Sophonisba,* 'The winged vengeance of incensed *Jove*' (Wood,
II.10).

If blood, heart, brain, plot ought save vengeance!
Mar. Wilt thou to bed? I wonder when thou sleep'st.
    I'faith thou look'st sunk-eyed; go, couch thy head;
    Now faith, 'tis idle; sweet, sweet son, to bed.
Ant. I have a prayer or two to offer up   45
    For the good, good prince, my most dear, dear lord,
    The duke Piero, and your virtuous self;
    And then when those prayers have obtained success,
    In sooth I'll come—believe it now—and couch
    My head in downy mould; but first I'll see   50
    You safely laid. I'll bring ye all to bed,
    Piero, Maria, Strotzo, Julio,
    I'll see you all laid; I'll bring you all to bed,
    And then, i'faith, I'll come and couch my head
    And sleep in peace.
Mar.   Look then, we go before.   55

Exeunt all but ANTONIO.

Ant. Ay, so you must, before we touch the shore
    Of wished revenge. O, you departed souls
    That lodge in coffined trunks which my feet press—
    If Pythagorean axioms be true,
    Of spirit's transmigration—fleet no more   60
    To human bodies! rather live in swine,
    Inhabit wolves' flesh, scorpions, dogs and toads,
    Rather than man. The curse of heaven rains
    In plagues unlimited through all his days;
    His mature age grows only mature vice,   65
    And ripens only to corrupt and rot
    The budding hopes of infant modesty;
    Still striving to be more than man, he proves

52. Julio] *Hunter;* Luceo *Q.*   55. And ... before.] *so Hunter; two lines Q.*
63. rains] *Q;* raignes *1633;* reigns *Hunter.*

49–55.] An extensive *double-entendre*; Antonio intends to lead them to
their rooms and to their deaths.
59. *Pythagorean*] The belief that after death the souls of men may
inhabit animals.
60. *fleet*] pass away from the body.

More than a devil; devilish suspect,
Devilish cruelty, all hell-strained juice   70
Is pourèd to his veins, making him drunk
With fuming surquedries, contempt of heaven,
Untamed arrogance, lust, state, pride, murder.

Ghost of And. Murder. ⎫
Ghost of Fel. Murder. ⎬ *From above and beneath.*   75
Pan. Murder.   ⎭

Ant. Ay, I will murder; graves and ghosts
    Fright me no more; I'll suck red vengeance
    Out of Piero's wounds, Piero's wounds. [*Withdraws.*]

Enter two boys, with PIERO *in his nightgown and nightcap.*

Pie. Maria, love, Maria! She took this aisle.   80
    Left you her here? On, lights; away!
    I think we shall not warm our beds today.

Enter JULIO, FOROBOSCO, *and* CASTILIO.

Jul. Ho, father, father!
Pie. How now, Julio, my little pretty son?
    [*To* FOROBOSCO] Why suffer you the child to walk so
        late?   85
For. He will not sleep, but calls to follow you,
    Crying that bugbears and spirits haunted him.

ANTONIO *offers to come near and stab,*
PIERO *presently withdraws.*

69–73.] so *Hunter;* More . . . crueltie / All . . . vaines / Making . . . surquedries / Contempt . . . arrogance / Lust . . . murder *Q.*   70. hell-
strained] *Bullen;* hell-straid *Q.*   73. S.H.] *Bullen; And. Q.*   75. S.H.]
Bullen; Fel. Q.   76. Ay] *Keltie;* I *Q.*   79. *Withdraws.*] *This ed., Bullen
subst.*   80. aisle] *Keltie;* Ile *Q.*

---

70. *hell-strained*] Q's 'hell-straid' is also missing from *O.E.D.* Q might
mean 'strayed from hell', but Bullen's emendation, 'strained through hell',
makes convincing sense; see Cross, *N. & Q.*, 206, 124.
    72. *fuming surquedries*] raging arrogance.
    74–6.] Cf. *Ham.*, I.v.144 ff.

Ant. [*Aside*] No, not so,
    This shall be sought for; I'll force him feed on life
    Till he shall loathe it. This shall be the close   90
    Of vengeance' strain.
Pie. Away there! Pages, lead on fast with light.
    The church is full of damps, 'tis yet dead night.
                    Exeunt all, saving JULIO [*and* ANTONIO].

SCENE III.

Jul. Brother Antonio, are you here i'faith?
    Why do you frown? Indeed my sister said
    That I should call you brother, that she did,
    When you were married to her. Buss me, good;
    'Truth, I love you better than my father, 'deed.   5
Ant. Thy father? Gracious, O bounteous heaven!
    I do adore thy justice: *venit in nostras manus*
    Tandem vindicta, venit et tota quidem.
Jul. 'Truth, since my mother died I loved you best.
    Something hath angered you; pray you, look merrily.   10
Ant. I will laugh and dimple my thin cheek
    With cap'ring joy; chuck, my heart doth leap
    To grasp thy bosom. [*Embraces* JULIO.] Time, place
    and blood,

93.1. *Exeunt*] *Bullen; Exit Q.*
Scene III] SCENA TERTIA *Q; not in Keltie, Bullen, Hunter.*
4–5. good; / 'Truth, I] *This ed.;* good / Truth, I *Q;* good truth, / I
Bullen, Hunter.   8.] *Hunter adds* [*Holds* Julio].

88.] *Cf.* this decision by Antonio to delay his vengeance, although he has
an opportunity to slay Piero, with Hamlet's decision in III.iii.
    90–1. *the close . . . strain*] i.e. the unifying cadence to conclude the
melody of vengeance.
    93. *damps*] *cf.* I.iii.74 n.
    III.iii. 1. *Brother*] i.e. brother-in-law.
    4. *Buss*] kiss.
    7–8. venit . . . quidem] Seneca, *Thyestes*, 494–5 (Marston substitutes
'vindicta' for 'Thyestes'), 'At length has vengeance come into my power,
and that to the full' (trans. Keltie).

How fit you close together! Heaven's tones
Strike not such music to immortal souls　　　　　　15
As your accordance sweets my breast withal.
Methinks I pace upon the front of Jove,
And kick corruption with a scornful heel,
Griping this flesh, disdain mortality.
O that I knew which joint, which side, which limb　　20
Were father all, and had no mother in't,
That I might rip it vein by vein and carve revenge
In bleeding rases! But since 'tis mixed together,
Have at adventure, pell-mell, no reverse—
Come hither, boy. This is Andrugio's hearse.　　　25

　　　　　[ANTONIO *draws his dagger.*]

Jul. O God, you'll hurt me. For my sister's sake,
　　Pray you do not hurt me. And you kill me, 'deed,
　　I'll tell my father.
Ant. O, for thy sister's sake I flag revenge. [*Enter Ghost.*]
Ghost of And. Revenge!　　　　　　　　　　30
Ant. Stay, stay, dear father, fright mine eyes no more.
　　Revenge as swift as lightning bursteth forth
　　And clears his heart. [*Exit Ghost.*] Come, pretty, tender child,
　　It is not thee I hate, not thee I kill.
　　Thy father's blood that flows within thy veins　　35
　　Is it I loathe, is that revenge must suck.

21. in't,] *Halliwell;* in't: *Q;* in't *Hunter.*　　24. pell-mell] pel mell *Q.*
30. S.H.] *Bullen; And. Q.*　　33. clears] *Q;* cleaves *Bullen, Wood, Hunter.*
33. S.D.] *This ed.; Hunter places after l. 30.*

---

14. *How fit you close*] How well you harmonise.
16. *accordance*] agreement, harmonious cord.
17. *front*] brow; cf. *Ham.*, III.iv.56, 'the front of Jove himself'.
19. *this flesh*] Julio's.
23. *rases*] cuts, slits, scratches.
24. *at adventure*] at hazard (i.e. recklessly).
no reverse] no retreat.
29. *I flag*]* i.e. I allow my revenge to delay (*O.E.D.*, *vb.*[1] 4).
33. *clears his heart*] i.e. relieves Andrugio's spirit of its discontent at the delay in the execution of the revenge.

I love thy soul, and were thy heart lapped up
In any flesh but in Piero's blood
I would thus kiss it; but being his, thus, thus,
And thus I'll punch it. [*Stabs* JULIO.] Abandon fears;   40
Whilst thy wounds bleed, my brows shall gush out tears.
Jul. So you will love me, do even what you will.
Ant. Now barks the wolf against the full-cheeked moon,
Now lions' half-clammed entrails roar for food,
Now croaks the toad and night-crows screech aloud,   45
Fluttering 'bout casements of departing souls;
Now gapes the graves, and through their yawns let loose
Imprisoned spirits to revisit earth.
And now swart night, to swell thy hour out,
Behold I spurt warm blood in thy black eyes.   50

[ANTONIO *holds up* JULIO'S *body.*]
From under the stage a groan.

Howl not thou pury mould, groan not ye graves,
Be dumb all breath. Here stands Andrugio's son,
Worthy his father. So; I feel no breath;
His jaws are fallen, his dislodged soul is fled,
And now there's nothing but Piero left.   55
He is all Piero, father, all; this blood,

---

40. S.D.] *so this ed.; Bullen delays the stabbing to the end of l. 50.*   43. full-
cheeked] full cheekt *Q*.

---

43. *wolf . . . moon*] Possibly proverbial; *cf.* Tilley, D.449, 'The Wolf
barks in vain at the moon'.
44. *half-clammed*]* Probably formed from 'clam' (*O.E.D.*, *vb.*[1] 2) 'to
stick or plaster up together' (i.e. half stuck through starvation) (?)
parodied by Jonson, *Poet.*, I.ii.184–6, 'What / will he clem me, and my
followers? Aske him, an' he will / clem me'.
45. *night-crows*] Probably owls or nightjars, and virtually synonymous
with 'night raven', a bird believed to be able to smell death; *cf.* Spenser,
S.C., June 23–4, 'Here no night Ravens lodge more black then pitche, /
Nor elvish ghosts, nor gastly owles doe flee'; see I.i.7 n.
47. *yawns*]* gaping openings (*O.E.D.*, *sb.* I).
51. *pury mould*]* decomposed matter: *O.E.D.* cites this as the only
example of 'pury' meaning rotten.

This breast, this heart, Piero all,
Whom thus I mangle. Sprite of Julio,
Forget this was thy trunk. I live thy friend.
Mayst thou be twinèd with the soft'st embrace   60
Of clear eternity; but thy father's blood
I thus make incense of: [ANTONIO *allows* JULIO'S *blood*
to fall upon the hearse.] to Vengeance!
Ghost of my poisoned sire, suck this fume;
To sweet revenge, perfume thy circling air
With smoke of blood. I sprinkle round his gore   65
And dew thy hearse with these fresh-reeking drops.
Lo, thus I heave my blood-dyed hands to heaven,
Even like insatiate hell, still crying; 'More!
My heart hath thirsting dropsies after gore.'
Sound peace and rest to church, night-ghosts and graves;   70
Blood cries for blood, and murder murder craves.

                                              [*Exit.*]

SCENE IV.
Enter two Pages with torches, MARIA, *her hair loose,*
and NUTRICHE.

Nut. Fie, fie, tomorrow your wedding day and weep! God's
   my comfort, Andrugio could do well, Piero may do
   better. I have had four husbands myself. The first I
   called 'Sweet Duck', the second 'Dear Heart', the third

---

62. incense of: [ANTONIO . . . *hearse*] to vengeance!] *so this ed.;* incense of,
to vengeance. *Q;* incense of to vengeance. *Bullen*; incense of, to Vengeance.
[*Sprinkles the tomb with blood.*] *Hunter.*   66. fresh-reeking] fresh reeking
Q.   67. blood-dyed] blood-died *Q.*   70. night-ghosts] night ghosts *Q.*
Scene IV] SCENA QVARTA *Q;* SCENE II *Keltie, Bullen, Hunter.*

---

   69. *thirsting dropsies*] diseased like dropsy and thus full of water, but still
thirsty.
   71.] Tilley, B.458, 'Blood will have blood', a common proverb.
   III.iv. 3–6.] Crispinella in *Dutch C.*, III.i.129–31, dismisses similar terms
of affection: 'call him not love: 'tis the drab's phrase; nor sweet honey, nor
my cony, nor dear duckling: 'tis the citizen terms'.

'Pretty Pug'; but the fourth, most sweet, dear, pretty,   5
all in all; he was the very cockall of a husband. What,
lady? Your skin is smooth, your blood warm, your
cheek fresh, your eye quick; change of pasture makes fat
calves, choice of linen clean bodies; and—no question!
—variety of husbands perfect wives. I would you should   10
know it, as few teeth as I have in my head, I have read
Aristotle's *Problems*, which saith that woman receiveth
perfection by the man. What then be the men? Go to,
to bed; lie on your back; dream not on Piero, I say no
more; tomorrow is your wedding; do, dream not of   15
Piero.

Enter BALURDO *with a bass viol.*

Mar. What an idle prate thou keep'st! Good nurse, go sleep.
        I have a mighty task of tears to weep.
Bal. Lady, with a most retort and obtuse leg,
        I kiss the curlèd locks of your loose hair. [*Bows.*]   20

---

13. then be] *Q;* then by *Hunter.*   19–20. Lady . . . leg, / I . . . hair.] *so*
Bullen; prose in Q.

---

5. *Pug*] A term of endearment.
6. *cockall*]* one that beats all, the 'perfection' (with an ironic implication?). This is the only usage cited by *O.E.D.*; Marston may have
developed the word from the Italian *coccale, 'a gull, a ninnie, a sot, such a
one as will beleeve the moone is made of greene cheese'.* Nutriche found her
fourth husband the best, as he was the easiest to deceive.
8–9. *change . . . calves*] Proverbial; Tilley, c.230.
12. *Aristotle's* Problems] A chap-book of questions and answers on
topics in popular science, mainly human physiology, e.g. 'Averrois doth
say, that the wombe & nature doe draw the seede, as the Lodestone doth
yron, and the Agathe steele: but she dooth draw it for the perfection of
herself', *The Problems of Aristotle* (1595 edn.), sig. E3; and *cf.* Shirley, *The
Ball*, 'Lucina. I'll fetch you a book to swear by. / *Winfield.* Let it be Venus
and Adonis then, / Or Ovid's wanton Elegies, Aristotle's / Problems, Guy
of Warwick, or sir Beavis' (*Works*, ed. Gifford and Dyce, III.71–2).
13. *be the men*] Q's 'be' (implying that men are beyond superlatives)
makes good sense. Hunter's 'by' is thus unnecessary.
17. *prate*] chatter.
19. *retort and obtuse*] Cf. I.iii.22; one of Balurdo's catch phrases.
leg] bow.

The Duke hath sent you the most musical Sir Geoffrey,
with his not base but most ennobled viol, to rock your
baby thoughts in the cradle of sleep.

Mar. I give the noble Duke respective thanks.

Bal. 'Respective'; truly a very pretty word. Indeed, Madam,   25
I have the most respective fiddle. [*Plucks it.*] Did you
ever smell a more sweet sound ? My ditty must go thus—
[*Plays.*] very witty I assure you. I myself in an humorous passion made it to the tune of 'My Mistress
Nutriche's beauty'. Indeed, very pretty, very retort and   30
obtuse, I'll assure you. 'Tis thus: [*Recites.*]
    My mistress' eye doth oil my joints
    And makes my fingers nimble;
    O love, come on, untruss your points,
    My fiddlestick wants rosin.   35
    My lady's dugs are all so smooth
    That no flesh must them handle;
    Her eyes do shine, for to say sooth,
    Like a new-snuffed candle.

Mar. Truly, very pathetical and unvulgar.   40

Bal. 'Pathetical' and 'unvulgar'; words of worth, excellent
words. In sooth, madam, I have taken a murr, which
makes my nose run most pathetically and unvulgarly.
Have you any tobacco ?

29–30. 'My . . . beauty'] *This ed.*; my mistresse *Nutriches* beautie Q.   31.
you. 'Tis] *Bullen subst.*, *Hunter;* you tis Q.   35.] *Q prints as part of song;*
Hunter prints as interpolated remark.   39. new-snuffed] newe snuffed Q.

24. *respective*] courteous; Balurdo goes on to misuse the word. Shakespeare uses the same comic technique of the misuse of words in *LLL.*
III.i, and *Tw.N.*, I.iii.

28–9. *humorous passion*] a passionate mood.

34. *untruss your points*] unfasten your clothes.

35. *rosin*] resin (i.e. it squeaks).

40. *pathetical and unvulgar*] moving and refined.

42. *a murr*] an attack of catarrh.

43. *unvulgarly*] remarkably; Balurdo again misuses a word introduced
by a courtier; *cf.* l. 25 above, 'respective'.

44. *tobacco*] i.e. snuff. Tobacco is 'verie good and holsome for those men
that are of moist constitutions: for he that is of this temperature, hath a

Mar. Good signior, your song.   45
Bal. Instantly, most unvulgarly, at your service. Truly, here's
    the most pathetical rosin. Umh.

They sing.

Mar. In sooth, most knightly sung, and like Sir Geoffrey.
Bal. Why, look you, lady, I was made a knight only for my
    voice, and a councillor only for my wit.   50
Mar. I believe it. Good night, gentle sir, good night.
Bal. You will give me leave to take my leave of my mistress,
    and I will do it most famously in rhyme:
Farewell, adieu, saith thy love true,
As to part loath.   55

47.1. *They sing*] *This ed.; Cantant Q; A Song Bullen; Cantat Hunter.*
49. made] *1633;* wade *Q.*   51. Good . . . good] *1633;* God . . . god *Q.*

---

bodie soft, not rugged and rough, white skinned; his veines and ioynts not
standing out, nor greatly appearing; his haire plaine and flat, and for the
most part thick withall. Their taste and smelling, and other obiects of their
senses be blunt and grosse. And if withall they be cold, they are for the
most part, in minde and wit doltish and dull, slouthfull and lumpish:
finally, neither by nature, neither by use, fore-castfull, sharpe-witted, nor
craftie: by reason their naturall heat is languishing and feeble, and
drowned with moist & cold humors: and therefore also their memorie is
verie faileable, oblivious, & nothing at all (in a manner) retentive. Their
speach, as likewise their pulses, and manner of gate, slowe and dull. And
because commonly they be assailed with many and sundry diseases, for
that they be given to sit still, loving their ease and idleness, whereby many
crude and raw humors are heaped up in their bodies, it must needs be
graunted that Tabacco being hot and drie in qualitie, must of necessitie do
them much good' (E. Gardiner, *The triall of tobacco* (1610), *sig.* Ev).
Balurdo is, then, right to ask for tobacco as a medicine.

    47. *rosin*] resin; used figuratively to mean the sound produced by the
resin, the song.
    47.1.] Presumably Balurdo and the Pages sing, perhaps accompanied by
the choir.
    49–50.] Rossaline made Balurdo a knight of the golden harp after he
sang a song (*I Ant. & Mel.*, v.ii.28), and he was thus made a knight only
for his voice.
    55.] 'A *Loth to depart* was the common term for a song sung or a tune
played on taking leave of friends' (*Old English Popular Music*, W. Chappell,
rev. H. E. Woolridge, New York, 1961, I.102).

Time bids us part, mine own sweetheart,
    God bless us both.   *Exit* BALURDO.
Mar. Good night, Nutriche. Pages, leave the room.
    The life of night grows short, 'tis almost dead.
                                    Exeunt Pages and NUTRICHE.
    O thou cold widow-bed, sometime thrice blest   60
    By the warm pressure of my sleeping lord,
    Open thy leaves, and whilst on thee I tread
    Groan out, 'Alas, my dear Andrugio's dead!'

MARIA *draweth the curtain, and the Ghost of* ANDRUGIO
        is displayed sitting on the bed.

    Amazing terror, what portent is this?

SCENE V.

Ghost of And. Disloyal to our hym'neal rites,
    What raging heat reigns in thy strumpet blood?
    Hast thou so soon forgot Andrugio?
    Are our love-bands so quickly cancellèd?
    Where lives thy plighted faith unto this breast?   5
    O weak Maria! Go to, calm thy fears;
    I pardon thee, poor soul. [MARIA *weeps.*] O, shed no tears;
    Thy sex is weak. That black incarnate fiend
    May trip thy faith, that hath o'erthrown my life.
    I was empoisoned by Piero's hand.   10

60. widow-bed] widdowe bed *Q.*

Scene v] SCENA QVINTA *Q; not in Keltie, Bullen, Hunter.*   1. S.H.]
Bullen; And. Q.   7. S.D.] *so this ed.; Hunter adds* [*She weeps.*] *after l. 5.*

---

59. *dead*] ended.

III.v. This scene of the revenger, the ghost of the murdered father and
his widow, who is contemplating remarriage to his murderer, compares
with the same situation in *Ham.*, III.iv. In Shakespeare's version, however,
the ghost is visible only to the revenger.

1. *hym'neal*]* of marriage (*O.E.D.*, A. *adj.*); *cf. What You Will*, Wood,
II.293, 'tooke my leave with Hymeneall rights'.

10. *empoisoned*]* killed by poison (*O.E.D.*, *ppl. a*); *cf. Malcontent*,
v.vi.34-5, 'she hath empoisoned / The reverend hermit'.

Join with my son to bend up strained revenge;
Maintain a seeming favour to his suit
Till time may form our vengeance absolute.

Enter ANTONIO, *his arms bloody,* [*bearing*] *a torch and
a poniard.*

Ant. See, unamazed I will behold thy face,
Outstare the terror of thy grim aspect,   15
Daring the horrid'st object of the night.
Look how I smoke in blood, reeking the steam
Of foaming vengeance. O, my soul's enthroned
In the triumphant chariot of revenge.
Methinks I am all air and feel no weight   20
Of human dirt clog. This is Julio's blood;
Rich music, father! this is Julio's blood.
Why lives that mother? [*Pointing to* MARIA.]
Ghost of And.   Pardon ignorance.
Fly, dear Antonio.
Once more assume disguise, and dog the court   25
In feignèd habit till Piero's blood
May even o'erflow the brim of full revenge.
Peace and all blessed fortunes to you both.
[*To* ANTONIO] Fly thou from court; be peerless in revenge.
Exit ANTONIO.
[*To* MARIA] Sleep thou in rest; lo, here I close thy
couch.   30
Exit MARIA *to her bed,* ANDRUGIO *drawing the curtains.*
And now, ye sooty coursers of the night,

24. S.H.] *Bullen; And. Q.*   29.1. *Exit* ANTONIO] *So Bullen; Q prints*
after l. 28.

---

11. *bend . . . revenge*] i.e. to lift up the head of Vengeance, bent under the
weight of the burden of duty; *cf.* III.i.46.
13.1.] *Cf.* Piero at I.i.0.1–2.
18. *foaming*] See II.ii.21 n.
23. *Pardon ignorance*] Forgive your mother, for she did not understand
how Piero had deceived her.
26. *feignèd habit*] Antonio enters at IV.i in a 'fool's habit'.

Hurry your chariot into hell's black womb.
Darkness, make flight; graves, eat your dead again;
Let's repossess our shrouds. Why lags delay?
Mount, sparkling brightness, give the world his day.   35

Exit ANDRUGIO.

The Third Act is Concluded.

35.2.] *This ed.; Explicit Actus tertius. Q.*

---

33. *eat your dead again*] Spirits return to their graves at first light.

Act IV

SCENE I.

Enter ANTONIO *in a fool's habit, with a little toy of a walnut
shell and soap to make bubbles;* MARIA *and* ALBERTO.

Mar. Away with this disguise in any hand!
Alb. Fie, 'tis unsuiting to your elate spirit.
　　　Rather put on some trans-shaped cavalier,
　　　Some habit of a spitting critic, whose mouth
　　　Voids nothing but gentle and unvulgar　　　　　　　5
　　　Rheum of censure; rather assume—
Ant. Why then should I put on the very flesh
　　　Of solid folly. No, this coxcomb is a crown
　　　Which I affect, even with unbounded zeal.
Alb. 'Twill thwart your plot, disgrace your high resolve.　　10
Ant. By wisdom's heart, there is no essence mortal
　　　That I can envy, but a plump-cheeked fool.

IV.i.3. trans-shaped] transshap't *Q*.　　12. plump-cheeked] plumpe cheekt
Q.

IV. This act takes place 'within', during the hours of daylight.

1. *in any hand*] at any rate, in any case.

2. *elate*] exalted, proud; *cf. I Ant. & Mel.*, Ind., 8–9, 'thus frame your
exterior shape / To haughty form of elate majesty'.

3. *trans-shaped*]* transformed (*O.E.D.*, *ppl. a*); i.e. put on the dress of a
courtier who has fallen on hard times.

4. *habit*] dress.
　spitting] malicious.

5. *Voids*] empties out.
　gentle and unvulgar] sweet and refined; *cf.* III.iv.40.

6. *Rheum*] catarrh: *cf. Ham.*, II.ii.499–500, 'threat'ning the flames / With
bisson rheum,' and Marston, *J. Drum's Ent.*, 'salt rheume' (Wood, III.221).

8. *coxcomb*] i.e. the fool's cap he is wearing.

12. *plump-cheeked*] *Cf. What You Will*, 'good plump cheekt chub'
(Wood, II.252).

O, he hath a patent of immunities,
Confirmed by custom, sealed by policy,
As large as spacious thought.   15
Alb. You cannot press among the courtiers
          And have access to—
Ant. What! Not a fool ? Why, friend, a golden ass,
          A baubled fool are sole canonical,
          Whilst pale-cheeked wisdom and lean-ribbed art   20
          Are kept in distance at the halberd's point,
          All held Apocrypha, not worth survey.
          Why, by the genius of that Florentine,
          Deep, deep-observing, sound-brained Machiavel,

---

19. baubled] *Hunter;* babl'd *Q.*   20. pale-cheeked ... lean-ribbed] pale
cheekt . . . leane ribd *Q.*   24. deep-observing, sound-brained] deepe
observing, sound brain'd *Q.* Machiavel] *Bullen;* Macheueil *Q.*

13–15. *he hath . . . thought*] He has permission to speak his mind
unpunished—a right confirmed by common acceptance and guaranteed by
the self-interest of statesmen, a right which is as extensive as the unlimited
extent of thought itself.

18. *a golden ass*] a wealthy fool.

19. *baubled*]* having a bauble or fool's baton: probably conflated with
'babble', to talk childishly, to prattle.

sole canonical] the only ones accepted as authoritative.

20. *art*] learning.

21. *halberd's*] as carried by Castilio, Forobosco, Alberto and Balurdo,
III.i.o.1; a poleaxe.

22. *Apocrypha*] The uncanonical books of the Bible, hence 'spurious'.

24. *sound-brained*] Cf. 'this weak-brain'd duke', *Malcontent*, III.iii.81.

Machiavel] Niccolo Di Machiavelli, the Florentine (1469–1527), was
best known in England for his work *The Prince* (written in 1513), a
manual of advice to sovereigns. Marston gives the impression of being
familiar with Machiavelli's work in Italian, and Antonio's admiration for
his political astuteness is a more balanced judgement than that commonly
found in Elizabethan drama (*cf.*, Marlowe, *Jew of Malta*, Prologue) which
tended to be derived from Gentillet's *Contre-Machiavel* (1576), a violent
indictment. Gentillet assumes that Machiavelli advocated 'crueltie,
perfidie, craft, perjurie, impietie, revenges, contempt of counsell and
friends, entertainment of flatterers, tromperie, the hatred of vertue,
covetousness, inconstancie and other like vices' (trans. Paterick, 1602, p.
348). Marston may be seeking to establish a contrast between Piero (the
villain of Gentillet's description) and Antonio (the politician of the true
Machiavellian persuasion).

He is not wise that strives not to seem fool.   25
When will the Duke hold fee'd intelligence,
Keep wary observation in large pay,
To dog a fool's act?
Mar. Ay, but such feigning, known, disgraceth much.
Ant. Pish! Most things that morally adhere to souls   30
Wholly exist in drunk opinion,
Whose reeling censure, if I value not,
It values nought.
Mar. You are transported with too slight a thought,
If you but meditate of what is past   35
And what you plot to pass.
Ant. Even in that, note a fool's beatitude:
He is not capable of passion;
Wanting the power of distinction,
He bears an unturned sail with every wind;   40
Blow east, blow west, he stirs his course alike.
I never saw a fool lean; the chub-faced fop

25. He is] *1633;* He is is *Q.*

25.] *Cf.* Machiavelli, *Discourses,* III.2, *It is very wise to pretend madness at the right time;* 'You must . . . play the fool like Brutus, and often you play the madman, praising, speaking, seeing, and doing things contrary to your purpose, to please the prince' (trans. A. Gilbert, Durham, N.C., 1965, I).

26. *hold . . . intelligence*] pay secret police.

30. *Pish !*] A common exclamation of disgust or impatience; *cf. J. Drum's Ent.,* Wood, III.189, 'Pish, by my maiden-head'.

morally] as a product of the moral sense.

31. *drunk opinion*] the brash ignorance of the vulgar; Marston ironically dedicates *The Metamorphosis of Pigmalions Image* to 'The Worlds Mightie Monarch, Good Opinion'.

32. *reeling censure*] fluctuating judgement.

34–6.] If you pause to consider what you have done in the past and what you are planning to do in the future, you will realise that you have deluded yourself with this notion of disguising yourself as a fool.

42. *chub-faced*] round-cheeked (*O.E.D.,* 'chub' 4. *b. Comb.*).

42–5.] Hunter (*N. & Q.,* N.S., 19 (1972), 452) compares Erasmus, *Encomium Moriae (Opera Omnia,* IV (1703), 415A) trans. Challoner (*E.E.T.S.,* 257 (1965), 19), '. . . sharp travailing of the brain by little and little soaking up the lively juice of the spirits; whereas my fools, on the other side, be sleek and smooth skinned'.

Shines sleek with full-crammed fat of happiness,
Whilst studious contemplation sucks the juice
From wizards' cheeks, who, making curious search   45
For nature's secrets, the first innating cause
Laughs them to scorn as man doth busy apes
When they will zany men. Had heaven been kind,
Creating me an honest, senseless dolt,
A good, poor fool, I should want sense to feel   50
The stings of anguish shoot through every vein;
I should not know what 'twere to lose a father;
I should be dead of sense to view defame
Blur my bright love; I could not thus run mad
As one confounded in a maze of mischief   55
Staggered, stark felled with bruising stroke of chance;
I should not shoot mine eyes into the earth,
Poring for mischief that might counterpoise

Enter LUCIO.

Mischief, murder and—How now, Lucio?
Luc. My lord, the Duke with the Venetian states   60
   Approach the great hall to judge Mellida.
Ant. Asked he for Julio yet?
Luc. No motion of him. Dare you trust this habit?

43. full-crammed] full cramm'd *Q.*

---

45. *wizard's*] wise men; *cf.* Milton, *Nativity Ode*, l. 23, 'The Star-led Wizards'.
   46. *the first . . . cause*]* i.e. the Prime Mover, God.
   46–8.] *Cf.* Milton, *Paradise Lost*, VIII.76–82, '. . . he [God] his Fabric of the Heav'ns / Hast left to thir disputes, perhaps to move / His Laughter at thir quaint Opinions wide / Hereafter, when they come to model Heav'n / And calculate the Stars, how they will wield / The mighty frame, how build, unbuild, contrive / To save appearances'.
   48. *zany*]* imitate awkwardly; *cf.* Florio, 'Zane . . . *a simple vice, clowne, foole, or simple fellowe in a plaie or comedie.*' Hunter compares the Zanni or clown of the Commedia dell'Arte.
   53.] i.e. I would be too insensitive to be aware how infamy . . .
   58. *poring*] searching.
   63. *motion*] suggestion, mention; i.e. there has been no question asked about him.

Ant. Alberto, see you straight rumour me dead.
    Leave me, good mother; leave me, Lucio;   65
    Forsake me all.   *Exeunt all, saving* ANTONIO.
        Now patience hoop my sides
    With steelèd ribs lest I do burst my breast
    With struggling passions. Now disguise stand bold!
    Poor scornèd habits oft choice souls enfold.

SCENE II.
The cornets sound a sennet.

Enter CASTILIO, FOROBOSCO, BALURDO, *and* ALBERTO *with poleaxes;* LUCIO *bare;* PIERO *and* MARIA *talking together; two Senators,* GALEATZO *and* MATZAGENTE, NUTRICHE.

Pie. [*To* MARIA]
    Entreat me not! There's not a beauty lives
    Hath that imperial predominance
    O'er my affects as your enchanting graces;
    Yet give me leave to be myself—
Ant. [*Aside*] A villain.
Pie.   Just—
Ant. [*Aside*]   Most just!   5
Pie. Most just and upright in our judgement seat.
    Were Mellida mine eye, with such a blemish
    Of most loathed looseness, I would scratch it out.

66. S.D.] *so Bullen; after* 'sides' *in Q.*   *Exeunt all*] *This ed.; Exeunt omnes Q.*
Scene II] SCENA SECVNDA *Q; not in Bullen, Hunter.*   0.1.] *after IV.i.70 in Q.*   5. [*Aside*] . . . just!] *so this ed.; three lines Q.*

---

64. *see . . . me*] i.e. see to it that straight away I am rumoured to be . . .
66. *hoop*] i.e. reinforce, like a barrel with iron bands.

IV.ii. 0.3. bare] i.e. without a hat.
2. *imperial*] with the power of an empress.
3. *affects*] feelings; *cf.* I.v.38.
    enchanting]* charming, enrapturing (*O.E.D., ppl. a.* 2).
    5. *Just . . . just*] Antonio takes Piero's *just* to mean 'correct', and seconds it as approving the description of him as a *villain.* Piero, of course, simply means 'righteous' (Hunter).

Produce the strumpet in her bridal robes,
That she may blush t'appear so white in show   10
And black in inward substance. Bring her in.
                    Exeunt FOROBOSCO *and* CASTILIO.
I hold Antonio, for his father's sake,
So very dearly, so entirely choice,
That knew I but a thought of prejudice
Imagined 'gainst his high ennobled blood   15
I would maintain a mortal feud, undying hate,
'Gainst the conceiver's life. And shall justice sleep
In fleshly lethargy for mine own blood's favour,
When the sweet prince hath so apparent scorn
By my—I will not call her daughter? Go;   20
Conduct in the loved youth Antonio.
                    Exit ALBERTO *to fetch* ANTONIO.
He shall behold me spurn my private good.
Piero loves his honour more than's blood.

Ant. [*Aside*] The devil he does, more than both.

Bal. Stand back there, fool; I do hate a fool most—most   25
pathetically. O, these that have no sap of—of retort and
obtuse wit in them—faugh!

Ant. [*Blowing bubbles.*] Puff! hold, world! Puff! hold, bubble!
Puff! hold, world! Puff! break not behind! Puff! thou
art full of wind; puff! keep up thy wind. Puff! 'tis   30
broke; and now I laugh like a good fool at the breath of
mine own lips: he, he, he, he, he.

Bal. You fool!

Ant.   You fool! Puff!

---

30. keep] *Q;* kept *Hunter* (*conj. Wood*).   thy] *Bullen;* by *Q.*   33. You
. . . Puff!] *so this ed.; two lines Q.*

---

13. *choice*] excellent.
18. *fleshly lethargy*] slothfulness of the flesh.
26. *pathetically*]* passionately, earnestly (*O.E.D.*, *adv.* 2).
28–33. *Puff!*] This is as much a stage direction as it is part of the
dialogue—Antonio punctuates his speech by blowing bubbles. One of the
characters in *J. Drum's Ent.* is called M. Puffe.

Bal. I cannot digest thee, the unvulgar fool. Go, fool.

Pie. Forbear, Balurdo; let the fool alone.   35

    (*Ficto.*) [*To* ANTONIO] Come hither. Is he your fool?

Mar. Yes, my loved lord.

Pie. [*Aside*] Would all the states in Venice were like thee:

    O then I were secured.

    He that's a villain or but meanly souled   40

    Must still converse and cling to routs of fools

    That cannot search the leaks of his defects.

    O, your unsalted fresh fool is your only man;

    These vinegar-tart spirits are too piercing,

    Too searching in the unglued joints of shaken wits.   45

    Find they a chink, they'll wriggle in and in,

    And eat like salt sea in his siddow ribs

    Till they have opened all his rotten parts

    Unto the vaunting surge of base contempt,

    And sunk the tossèd galleas in depth   50

    Of whirlpool scorn. Give me an honest fop—

    [*To* ANTONIO] Dud-a, dud-a. [*Gives him a gift.*]

        Why, lo, sir, this takes he

    As grateful now, as a monopoly.

---

34. the] *Q;* thou *Hunter.*   36.] *This ed.;* Come hither (*ficto*) Is he your foole? *Q.*   44. vinegar-tart] vinegar tart *Q.*   52. *Gives . . . gift.] Hunter subst.*

---

34. *unvulgar*] gentlemanly.

36. (Ficto.)] in an affected tone.

41. *routs*] disreputable crowd, a gang; *cf. What You Will*, 'to affright the rout / Of the Idolatrous vulgar' (Wood, II.260).

42. *search the leaks*] seek out the weak spots.

43. *unsalted*] without (sophisticated) spice.

45. *unglued*★ . . . *wits*] i.e. men lose their composure when subjected to too searching an interrogation into their motives.

47. *siddow*]★ soft, tender.

50. *galleas*] galleon.

52. *Dud-a*] (?) Piero uses childish babble to the childlike fool.

53. *monopoly*] economic privilege (normally the exclusive right to the sale of a particular commodity), granted by the monarch to members of the aristocracy. In the seventeenth century there was much public clamour against the granting of monopolies, and on 25 November 1601 Queen

SCENE III.

The still flutes sound softly.

Enter FOROBOSCO *and* CASTILIO; MELLIDA *supported by two waiting women.*

Mel. All honour to this royal confluence.

Pie. Forbear, impure, to blot bright honour's name
     With thy defilèd lips. The flux of sin
     Flows from thy tainted body. Thou so foul,
     So all-dishonoured, canst no honour give,   5
     No wish of good that can have good effect
     To this grave senate, and illustrate bloods.
     Why stays the doom of death?

1st Sen. Who riseth up to manifest her guilt?

2nd Sen. You must produce apparent proof, my lord.   10

Pie. Why, where is Strotzo, he that swore he saw
     The very act and vowed that Feliche fled
     Upon his sight? On which I break the breast
     Of the adulterous lecher with five stabs.
     [*To* CASTILIO] Go, fetch in Strotzo.
              [*To* MELLIDA] Now, thou impudent,   15

Scene III] SCENA TERTIA *Q; not in Keltie, Bullen, Hunter.*   5. all-dishonoured] all dishonour'd *Q*.

Elizabeth abolished them by proclamation, to forestall a Bill brought by the Commons against them. The proclamation was, however, ineffectual, as on 7 May 1603 James I suspended the operation of all monopolies; *cf.* Chapman, *Monsieur D'Olive* (1604), I.ii.94–5, 'monopolies are now called in, and wit's become a free trade for all sorts to live by.'

   IV.iii.0.I. still] soft, subdued.

   1. *confluence*] gathering; *cf.* Jonson, *Poet*, V.ii.40–1, 'The vast rude swinge of generall confluence / Is . . . exempt from sense'.

   3. *flux*] issue, discharge; *cf.* Jonson, *E.M. Out*, IV.viii.128, 'his disease is nothing but the *fluxe* of apparell'.

   7. *illustrate*] resplendent, illustrious; for the '-ate' suffix see I.i.104 n. and *I Ant. & Mel.*, II.i.109–10, 'your sweet self, than whom I know not a more exquisite, illustrate', where Forobosco uses it affectedly.

   bloods] families, stock.

   8. *stays*]* is long (in coming), *O.E.D., vb.*[1] 7. c.

   10. *apparent*] evident.

> If thou hast any drop of modest blood
> Shrouded within thy cheeks, blush, blush for shame
> That rumour yet may say thou felt'st defame.

Mel. Produce the devil; let your Strotzo come.
  I can defeat his strongest argument   20
  Which—

Pie.   With what?

Mel. With tears, with blushes, sighs and claspèd hands,
  With innocent upreared arms to heaven,
  With my unnooked simplicity. These, these
  Must, will, can only quit my heart of guilt; 25
  Heaven permits not taintless blood be spilt.
  If no remorse live in your savage breast—

Pie. Then thou must die.

Mel.   Yet dying, I'll be blest.

Pie. Accurst by me.

Mel.   Yet blest, in that I strove
  To live and die—

Pie.   My hate.

Mel.   Antonio's love. 30

Ant. [*Aside*] Antonio's love!

  Enter STROTZO, *a cord about his neck* [, *and* CASTILIO].

Str. O what vast ocean of repentant tears
  Can cleanse my breast from the polluting filth
  Of ulcerous sin? Supreme Efficient,
  Why cleavest thou not my breast with thunderbolts 35

---

21. Which . . . what?] *so this ed.; two lines* Q. Which] *Q;* With *Halliwell, Bullen.* 28–30. Then . . . blest. / Accurst . . . strove / To . . . love.] *so Hunter; seven lines* Q.

---

 18. *thou . . . defame*] i.e. that you were conscious of your disgrace.
 24. *unnooked*]* without any deception; probably a unique figurative usage of 'nooked'.
 34. *Supreme Efficient*] i.e. Prime Mover, God; *cf.* IV.i.46.
 35–6. *Why . . . revenge?*] The usual expression of displeasure by the gods of Greece or Rome.

Of winged revenge ?
Pie.   What means this passion ?
Ant. [*Aside*] What villainy are they decocting now ?
Umh!
Str. In me convertite ferrum, O proceres.
Nihil iste, nec ista.   40
Pie. Lay hold on him. What strange portent is this ?
Str. I will not flinch. Death, hell, more grimly stare
Within my heart than in your threat'ning brows.
Record, thou threefold guard of dreadest power,
What I here speak is forcèd from my lips   45
By the pulsive strain of conscience.
I have a mount of mischief clogs my soul
As weighty as the high-nolled Appennine;
Which I must straight disgorge or breast will burst.
I have defamed this lady wrongfully,   50
By instigation of Antonio,
Whose reeling love, tossed on each fancy's surge,
Began to loathe before it fully joyed.
Pie. Go, seize Antonio! Guard him strongly in!

                              Exit FOROBOSCO.

Str. By his ambition being only bribed,   55
Fee'd by his impious hand, I poisonèd
His agèd father, that his thirsty hope

---

36. Of . . . passion ?] *so Hunter; two lines Q.*   37–8. [*Aside*] . . . now ? /
Umh!] *so Hunter; one line Q.*   46. pulsive] *Q;* impulsive *Bullen, Hunter.*
54.1.] *so Bullen; Q prints after l. 53.*   57. hope] *Q;* hopes *Bullen, Hunter.*

---

37. *decocting*]* devising, concocting (*O.E.D., vb.* 6. *fig.*).

39–40.] i.e. 'Turn the sword on me, O nobles! Neither he nor she has
done anything'; based upon Virgil, *Aen.,* IX.427–8.

44. *threefold guard*] Probably Cerberus, the three-headed watchdog of
Hades who ate spirits who tried to leave the underworld.

46. *pulsive*]* constraining, compelling (*O.E.D., a.* 1).

48. *high-nolled*] high-peaked (*O.E.D.,* 'nolled' *a*).

53. *joyed*] enjoyed.

57–9. *that . . . quaff*] i.e. that his desire to be king might find its insatiable
craving quenched by the boundless satisfaction available to an absolute
monarch.

Might quench their dropsy of aspiring drought
With full unbounded quaff.
Pie. Seize me Antonio!   60
Str. O why permit you now such scum of filth
As Strotzo is to live and taint the air
With his infectious breath?
Pie. Myself will be thy strangler, unmatched slave.

PIERO *comes from his chair, snatcheth the cord's end and* CASTILIO
aideth him; both strangle STROTZO.

Str. Now change your—
Pie.   Ay, pluck, Castilio!   65
I change my humour! Pluck, Castilio!
Die, with thy death's entreats even in thy jaws!
Now, now, now, now. [*Aside*] Now my plot begins to work.
Why, thus should statesmen do,
That cleave through knots of craggy policies,   70
Use men like wedges, one strike out another;
Till by degrees the tough and knurly trunk
Be rived in sunder. Where's Antonio?

Enter ALBERTO *running.*

Alb. O, black accursèd fate! Antonio's drowned.
Pie. Speak, on thy faith, on thy allegiance, speak!   75
Alb. As I do love Piero, he is drowned.

65. Ay, pluck, Castilio!] *so Keltie subst.;* I, pluck *Castilio Q;* I—pluck
Castilio! *Bullen.*   65–6. Now . . . Castilio! / I . . . Castilio!] *so Hunter;*
Now . . . your / I . . . humour? plucke / Castilio. *Q.*

58. *dropsy*] craving, insatiable thirst.
60. *me*] for me.
67. *death's entreats*] i.e. your appeal to be put to death.
70. *cleave*] cut; probably an allusion to cutting the Gordian knot; see
IV.v.88 n.
    craggy] hard to get through, because hard as a rock (*O.E.D. a.* 3. *fig.*).
71.] A similar image is used by Malevole: 'He would discharge us as
boys do eldern guns [popguns], one pellet to strike out another' (*Mal-content*, IV.iv.13–14).
72. *knurly*]* gnarled.

Ant. [*Aside*] In an inundation of amazement.

Mel. Ay, is this the close of all my strains in love ?
      O me, most wretched maid!

Pie. Antonio drowned ? How ? How ? Antonio drowned!   80

Alb. Distraught and raving, from a turret's top
      He threw his body in the high-swollen sea,
      And as he headlong topsy-turvy dinged down
      He still cried 'Mellida!'.

Ant. [*Aside*]   My love's bright crown!

Mel. He still cried 'Mellida' ?   85

Pie. Daughter, methinks your eyes should sparkle joy,
      Your bosom rise on tiptoe at this news.

Mel. Ay me!

Pie. How now, 'Ay me!' ? Why art not great of thanks
      To gracious heaven for the just revenge   90
      Upon the author of thy obloquies ?

Mar. [*Aside*] Sweet beauty, I could sigh as fast as you,
      But that I know that which I weep to know:
      His fortunes should be such he dare not show
      His open presence.   95

Mel. I know he loved me dearly, dearly I;
      And since I cannot live with him I die.

---

82. high-swollen] high swolne *Q.*   83. topsy-turvy] topsie turvie *Q.*
84. He . . . crown!] *so Hunter; two lines Q.*   84–5. 'Mellida!' . . . crown!
/ . . . Mellida ?] *so this ed.;* Mellida. / . . . crowne. / . . . *Mellida* ? *Q;*
"Mellida" . . . crown! / . . . "Mellida"! *Hunter.*

---

83. *dinged*] dashed violently; *cf. I Ant. & Mel.*, Ind., 84, 'And ding his
spirit to the verge of hell'; *cf.* also the description of a similar suicide-for-
love, *Malcontent*, IV.iii.1–50.

91. *obloquies*] disgrace: *cf.* II.ii.16 and *J. Drum's Ent.*, 'Leave *Brabant*
unto death, and obloquie' (Wood, III.231). In *I Ant. & Mel.*, II.i.159–61,
Piero sought to offer condolence to Mellida after a similar report that
Antonio had been drowned, by urging her to 'triumph' in his 'victories'
and to remember that 'the highborn bloods of Italy / Sue for thy seat of
love'.

94–5.] i.e. Antonio is in such disgrace that he cannot show himself
openly.

96. *dearly I*] i.e. I also loved him dearly.

Pie. 'Fore heaven, her speech falters; look she swoons.
　　　Convey her up into her private bed.

　　MARIA, NUTRICHE *and the Ladies bear out* MELLIDA, *as
　　　　　being swooned.*

　　　I hope she'll live. If not—　　　　　　　　　　100
Ant. [*Aside*] Antonio's dead!
　　　The fool will follow too. He, he, he!
　　　Now works the scene; quick observation scud
　　　To cote the plot, or else the path is lost;
　　　My very self am gone, my way is fled;　　　　105
　　　Ay, all is lost if Mellida is dead.　　　*Exit* ANTONIO.
Pie. Alberto, I am kind, Alberto, kind.
　　　I am sorry for thy coz, i'faith I am.
　　　Go, take him down and bear him to his father;
　　　Let him be buried; look ye, I'll pay the priest.　　　110
Alb. Please you to admit his father to the court?
Pie. No.
Alb. Please you to restore his lands and goods again?
Pie. No.
Alb. Please you vouchsafe him lodging in the city?　　　115
Pie. God's fut, no, thou odd uncivil fellow!
　　　I think you do forget, sir, where you are.
Alb. I know you do forget, sir, where you must be.
For. You are too malapert, i'faith you are.
　　　Your honour might do well to—　　　　　　　　120
Alb. Peace, parasite, thou bur, that only sticks

101–2. [*Aside*] . . . dead! / The fool . . . he!] *so this ed.; one line Q.*
104. cote] *Hunter;* coate *Q.*

　　103–4. *quick . . . plot*] i.e. let speedy observation hasten to discover the
way the plot is going to work out.
　　103. *scud*] dart; *cf. I Ant. & Mel.,* III.ii.261, 'fly, run post, scud away!'
　　104. *cote*] A coursing term, used figuratively; to outstrip, go beyond.
　　116. *fut*] foot.
　　118. *where you must be*] i.e. at the Last Judgement.
　　119. *malapert*] presumptuous.
　　121–2.] *Cf. What You Will,* 'an idle bur that stickst upon the nap of his
fortune' (Wood, II.272).

Unto the nap of greatness.

Pie. Away with that same yelping cur, away!

Alb. Ay, I am gone; but mark, Piero, this: 124
There is a thing called scourging Nemesis.   *Exit* ALBERTO.

Bal. God's neaks, he has wrong, that he has; and, 'sfut, and
I were as he, I would bear no coals. La, I—I begin to
swell—puff!

Pie. How now, fool, fop, fool!

Bal. Fool, fop, fool! Marry muff! I pray you, how many   130
fools have you seen go in a suit of satin? I hope yet I do
not look a fool i'faith. A fool! God's bores, I scorn't
with my heel. 'Sneaks, and I were worth but three
hundred pound a year more, I could swear richly; nay,
but as poor as I am, I will swear the fellow hath wrong.   135

Pie. [*Aside*] Young Galeatzo; ay, a proper man;
Florence, a goodly city; it shall be so.
I'll marry her to him instantly.
Then Genoa mine by my Maria's match,
Which I'll solemnize ere next setting sun;   140
Thus Venice, Florence, Genoa, strongly leagued.
Excellent, excellent! I'll conquer Rome,
Pop out the light of bright religion;
And then, helter-skelter, all cocksure!

---

130. S.H. *Bal.*] *1633; not in Q.*   144. helter-skelter] helter skelter *Q.*

125.] *Cf. Spanish Tragedy*, 'Well, heaven is heaven still, / And there is
Nemesis and Furies, / And things call'd whips' (Third Addition, ll. 40–2).

126. *God's neaks*] see II.i.54 n., and *cf.* Middleton, *A Trick to Catch the
Old One*, II.i.329–30, 'Coads nigs! I was never so disgraced since the /
hour my mother whipt me'.

'*sfut*] God's foot; *cf.* l. 116 above.

127. *I . . . coals*] i.e. I would not submit to this humiliation.

130. *Marry muff!*] An expression of contempt; *cf.* Middleton, *Blurt*,
'*Simperina.* How, sir, wearied? marry, foh! *Frisco.* Wearied, sir? marry
muff!' (II.ii.193).

130–1. *how . . . satin*] *Cf. The Famous Victories of Henry the Fifth*,
II.36–7, 'Am I a clown? Zounds, masters, do clowns go in silk apparel?'
(ed. S. M. Pitcher, New York, 1961).

133. *'Sneaks*] God's neaks; *cf.* l. 126 above.

Bal. Go to, 'tis just, the man hath wrong; go to.   145
Pie. Go to, thou shalt have right. Go to, Castilio,
　　　Clap him into the palace dungeon;
　　　Lap him in rags and let him feed on slime
　　　That smears the dungeon cheek. Away with him!
Bal. In very good truth now, I'll ne'er do so more; this one   150
　　　time and—
Pie. Away with him; observe it strictly, go!
Bal. Why then, O wight,
　　　Alas, poor knight!
　　　O, welladay,   155
　　　Sir Geofferey!
　　　Let poets roar,
　　　And all deplore;
　　　For now I bid you goodnight.

　　　　　　　　　　　　Exit BALURDO *with* CASTILIO.

[*Enter* MARIA.]

Mar. O piteous end of love! O too, too rude hand   160
　　　Of unrespective death! Alas, sweet maid!
Pie. Forbear me, heaven! What intend these plaints?
Mar. The beauty of admired creation,
　　　The life of modest, unmixed purity,
　　　Our sex's glory, Mellida is—   165

153–9. *so Bullen;* Why ... knight / O ... roare, / And ... night. *Q.*
159. goodnight] *1633;* god night *Q.*

153–9.] Balurdo's song is derived from a variety of sources. 'Welladay'
was a popular contemporary tune; a ballad to this tune and with the
refrain line 'Welladay! welladay!' was in circulation in 1601–02, entitled
'A lamentable Ditty composed upon the Death of Robert Lord Devereux,
late Earle of Essex, who was beheaded in the Tower of London, on
Ashwednesday in the morning, 1600' (i.e. 25 February 1601). This ballad
was often later printed with another, 'A Lamentable new Ballad upon the
Earle of Essex his Death', to the tune of 'Essex's last good night', which
had a refrain line ending in the word 'good-night' (*Roxburghe Ballads*,
1.564–74). Marston may have been influenced by Bottom's passion in
MND, v.i.268–9, 'But stay, O spite! / But mark, poor knight.'
　161. *unrespective*] inconsiderate (used seriously, but *cf.* III.iv.25).

Pie. What ? O heaven, what ?
Mar.   Dead!
Pie. May it not sad your thoughts, how ?
Mar. Being laid upon her bed, she grasped my hand,
　　And, kissing it, spake thus: 'Thou very poor,
　　Why dost not weep ? The jewel of thy brow,   170
　　The rich adornment that enchased thy breast,
　　Is lost; thy son, my love is lost, is dead.
　　And do I live to say Antonio's dead ?
　　And have I lived to see his virtues blurred
　　With guiltless blots ? O world, thou art too subtle   175
　　For honest natures to converse withal.
　　Therefore I'll leave thee. Farewell, mart of woe,
　　I fly to clip my love Antonio.'
　　With that her head sunk down upon her breast,
　　Her cheek changed earth, her senses slept in rest;   180
　　Until my fool, that pressed unto the bed,
　　Screeched out so loud that he brought back her soul,
　　Called her again, that her bright eyes 'gan ope
　　And stared upon him; he, audacious fool,
　　Dared kiss her hand, wished her soft rest, loved bride; 185
　　She fumbled out, 'thanks, good—' and so she died.
Pie. And so she died! I do not use to weep;
　　But by thy love (out of whose fertile sweet
　　I hope for as fair fruit) I am deep sad.
　　I will not stay my marriage for all this!   190

---

166. What ... Dead!] *so this ed.; two lines Q.*   190. I] *1633; not in Q.*

167.] i.e. if you can bear the pain which such an explanation must cause you.
171. *enchased*] set in (like a jewel).
175. *guiltless blots*] i.e. crimes of which he is not guilty.
176. *converse*] deal.
177. *mart*]* region, vale (*O.E.D.*, *sb.*⁴ 3. *transf.* and *fig.*).
180. *changed earth*] i.e. became dead.
188. *sweet*] embrace; *cf.* I.i.26.
190. *I*] A hiatus in Q indicates clearly that a one-letter word dropped out. Thus the reading of the 1633 edn. seems certain.
　stay] delay.

Castilio, Forobosco, all
Strain all your wits, wind up invention
Unto his highest bent; to sweet this night,
Make us drink Lethe by your quaint conceits,
That for two days oblivion smother grief;   195
But when my daughter's exequies approach,
Let's all turn sighers. Come, despite of fate,
Sound loudest music; let's pace out in state.
                    The cornets sound. Exeunt.

SCENE IV.
Enter ANTONIO *alone, in fool's habit.*

Ant. Ay, Heaven, thou mayst; thou mayst, Omnipotence.
What vermin bred of putrefacted slime
Shall dare to expostulate with thy decrees ?
O heaven, thou mayst indeed: she was all thine,
All heavenly, I did but humbly beg   5
To borrow her of thee a little time.
Thou gavest her me, as some weak-breasted dame
Giveth her infant, puts it out to nurse;
And when it once goes high-lone, takes it back.

Scene IV] SCENA QVARTA *Q;* Scene III *Keltie;* Scene II *Bullen, Hunter.*
0.1. *alone] Keltie; solus Q.*   7. weak-breasted] weake breasted *Q.*

192–5.] Strain to their limit your abilities to create diversions; so as to make this night delightful, use your power of amusing us to make us forget our sorrow.

194. *Lethe*] The river of the underworld, the waters of which brought forgetfulness.

196. *exequies*] funeral rites; *cf.* v.vi.43 and Shakespeare, *1H6*, III.ii.133, 'see his exequies fulfill'd'.

197. *sighers*]* people who sigh.

198. *in state*] in formal procession.

IV.iv. 1. *thou mayst*] i.e. allow such things as Mellida's death to occur.

2.] An allusion to the belief that life was spontaneously generated by the action of the sun upon decaying matter.

3. *expostulate*] remonstrate.

9. *high-lone*] quite alone, without support; *cf.* Middleton, *Blurt*, II.ii.26, 'when I could not stand a'high-lone without I held a thing'.

She was my vital blood; and yet, and yet,   10
I'll not blaspheme. Look here, behold!

ANTONIO *puts off his cap and lieth just upon his back.*

I turn my prostrate breast upon thy face
And vent a heaving sigh. O hear but this;
I am a poor, poor orphan; a weak, weak child,
The wrack of splitted fortune, the very ooze,   15
The quicksand that devours all misery.
Behold the valiant'st creature that doth breathe!
For all this I dare live, and I will live,
Only to numb some others' cursèd blood
With the dead palsy of like misery.   20
Then death, like to a stifling incubus,
Lie on my bosom. Lo, sir, I am sped:
My breast is Golgotha, grave for the dead.

SCENE V.

Enter PANDULPHO, ALBERTO *and a Page, carrying* FELICHE'S
trunk in a winding sheet, and lay it thwart ANTONIO'S *breast.*

Pan. Antonio, kiss my foot; I honour thee
    In laying thwart my blood upon thy breast.
    I tell thee boy, he was Pandulpho's son,
    And I do grace thee with supporting him.

Scene v] SCENA QVINTA *Q; not in Keltie, Bullen, Hunter.*

---

11. *blaspheme*] i.e. by remonstrating with heaven's decrees.
11.1.] *Cf.* Antonio's behaviour in *I Ant. & Mel.*, IV.i.164–5, when, while
grieving with Mellida, he cries, 'I am not for thee if thou canst not rave, /
ANTONIO *falls on the ground.* / Fall flat on the ground, and thus exclaim
on heaven.'
15. *The wrack . . . fortune*] 'the wreck left when the ship of fortune has
split open' (Hunter).
21. *incubus*] nightmare; *cf.* I.i.90 (used metaphorically).
23. *Golgotha*] John 19.17, 'And He bearing His cross went forth into a
place called *the place* of a skull, which is called in the Hebrew Golgotha'
(1611).
IV.v. 4. *supporting*] i.e. allowing you to support.

Young man,   5
The domineering monarch of the earth,
He who hath naught that fortune's gripe can seize,
He who is all impregnably his own,
He whose great heart heaven cannot force with force,
Vouchsafes his love. *Non servio Deo, sed assentio.*   10
Ant. I ha' lost a good wife.
Pan. Didst find her good, or didst thou make her good?
If found, thou mayst re-find, because thou hadst her:
If made, the work is lost; but thou that madest her
Livest yet as cunning. Hast lost a good wife?   15
Thrice blessed man that lost her whilst she was good,
Fair, young, unblemished, constant, loving, chaste,
I tell thee, youth, age knows young loves seem graced
Which with gray cares' rude jars are oft defaced.
Ant. But she was full of hope.   20
Pan. May be, may be; but that which 'may be' stood,

5–6. him. / Young man,] *so Bullen;* him, / Young man. *Q.*   6–7.] *so Q;*
Bullen transposes these lines.   13. re-find] refinde *Q.*

---

6. *domineering monarch*] the passionless Stoic.
10. Non . . . assentio] Seneca, *De Providentia*, v.6 (reading '*assentior*'):
'I am not slave to God, but give consent to his doings' (Hunter).
11–17.] Based upon Whyttynton's *Seneca*: '*Sensus.* Uxorem bonam
amisi. *Ratio.* Utrum bonam inueneris, aut feceras? Si inueneras, habere
te posse ex hoc intelligas licet habuisti. Si feceras, bene spera. Res periit:
saluus est artifex.' (*Sensualitie* [i.e. *Feeling*]. I have lost a good wife.
Reason. Whether dyd thou fynde her so, or dyd thou make her so? If thou
foundest her so, thou mayst knowe thou haste her styll so thoughe thou
haddest her: yf thou made her so, trust well of another. Thy good is lost,
but the worke man is safe . . . What doest thou prayse in her? *Sen.*
Chastyte and clene lyfe) (p. 61).
13. *re-find*]* find (one like her) again.
18–19.] i.e. young love loses its grace as a result of the trials and tribula-
tions of grey-haired age.
20–22.] From Whyttynton's *Seneca*: '*Sensualitie.* I have a good wyfe.
Reason. Yf thou had her thou can nat afferme for suerty that she wyll
contynue in that purpose: nothynge is so soone moved as a woman's wyll,
nothynge so unstable. *Sen.* But she was good and wolde have ben. *Re.*
Deth brought to passe, that thou may afferme that without damage' (p. 63).
21–2. *but . . . good*] i.e. when alive she was only potentially 'good', now
that she is dead (she died 'good') that potential is confirmed.

Stands now without all 'may'; she died good;
And dost thou grieve?

Alb.   I ha' lost a true friend.

Pan. I live encompassed with two blessèd souls!
      Thou lost a good wife; thou lost a true friend, ha?   25
      Two of the rarest lendings of the heavens;
      But lendings: which, at the fixed day of pay
      Set down by fate, thou must restore again.
      O what unconscionable souls are here!
      Are you all like the spoke-shaves of the church?   30
      Have you no maw to restitution?
      Hast lost a true friend, coz? Then thou hadst one.
      I tell thee, youth, 'tis all as difficult
      To find true friend in this apostate age
      (That balks all right affiance twixt two hearts)   35
      As 'tis to find a fixèd modest heart
      Under a painted breast. Lost a true friend?
      O happy soul that lost him whilst he was true.
      Believe it, coz, I to my tears have found,
      Oft dirt's respect makes firmer friends unsound.   40

Alb. You have lost a good son.

Pan. Why, there's the comfort on't, that he was good.
      Alas, poor innocent!

Alb.   Why weeps mine uncle?

---

23. And . . . friend] *so Hunter; two lines Q.*   43. Alas . . . uncle?] *so Hunter; two lines Q.*

23–5. *I . . . friend*] *Cf.* Whyttynton's *Seneca*: 'Sen. I have lost a frende.
Re. Have a bolde stomacke of many' (p. 59).

29. *Unconscionable*] without conscience.

30. *spoke-shaves*]* A carpenter's tool, used for planing curves; this
figurative usage probably refers to those who seek to gouge out lands and
wealth from the possessions of the church.

31.] i.e. Have you no inclination to give back what you ate up?

32.] From Whyttynton's *Seneca*: 'Sen. I have lost my frende. *Rea.* Nowe
it is certayne that thou had him' (p. 59).

35. *balks*] hinders, thwarts; *cf.* Jonson, *Poet.*, I.ii.217–18, 'Doe not balke
me, good swaggerer'.

40.] i.e. Often the desire for wealth makes firm friendship become
insecure.

Pan. Ha, dost ask me why ? ha ? ha ?
   Good coz, look here.   45

                 He shows him his son's breast.

   Man will break out, despite philosophy.
   Why, all this while I ha' but played a part,
   Like to some boy that acts a tragedy,
   Speaks burly words and raves out passion;
   But when he thinks upon his infant weakness,   50
   He droops his eye. I spake more than a god,
   Yet am less than a man.
   I am the miserablest soul that breathes.

                 ANTONIO *starts up.*

Ant. 'Slid, sir, ye lie! By th' heart of grief, thou liest!
   I scorn't that any wretched should survive   55
   Outmounting me in that superlative,
   Most miserable, most unmatched in woe.
   Who dare assume that, but Antonio ?
Pan. Will't still be so ? And shall yon bloodhound live ?
Ant. Have I an arm, a heart, a sword, a soul ?   60
Alb. Were you but private unto what we know!
Pan. I'll know it all; first, let's inter the dead;
   Let's dig his grave with that shall dig the heart,
   Liver and entrails of the murderer.

   They strike the stage with their daggers and the grave openeth.

Ant. [*To Page*] Will't sing a dirge, boy ?   65

47–51.] See Introduction, p. 38.
49. *burly*]* (of words, language) bombastic, inflated, turgid.
54. '*Slid*] God's lid (eyelid); *cf.* I.v.35.
55–7.] In *I Ant. & Mel.*, II.i.297, Antonio claims that he and Mellida
arc 'unmatch'd mirrors of calamity'.
56. *Outmounting*]* going beyond (*O.E.D.*, 'out' 18).
64.1.] *Cf. Spanish Tragedy*, III.xii.70–3, 'Hieronimo. Give me my son!
You shall not ransom him. / Away! I'll rip the bowels of the earth, / *He
diggeth with his dagger.* / And ferry over to th' Elysian plains, / And bring
my son to show his deadly wounds.'
65. Page] This is the boy who helped carry the body of Feliche, IV.v.o.1.

Pan. No; no song; 'twill be vile out of tune.
Alb. Indeed he's hoarse; the poor boy's voice is cracked.
Pan. Why, coz, why should it not be hoarse and cracked,
    When all the strings of nature's symphony
    Are cracked and jar? Why should his voice keep tune,   70
    When there's no music in the breast of man?
    I'll say an honest antique rhyme I have:
    Help me, good sorrow-mates, to give him grave.

      They all help to carry FELICHE *to his grave.*

    Death, exile, plaints and woe,
    Are but man's lackeys, not his foe.   75
    No mortal 'scapes from fortune's war
    Without a wound, at least a scar.
    Many have led these to the grave,
    But all shall follow, none shall save.
    Blood of my youth, rot and consume;   80
    Virtue, in dirt, doth life assume.
    With this old saw close up this dust:
    Thrice blessèd man that dieth just.
Ant. The gloomy wing of night begins to stretch

---

72. antique] *This ed.;* antick *Q;* antic *Bullen.*

---

72. *antique*] ancient; Q's 'antick' is simply a variant spelling. Bullen's 'antic' (grotesque) is unlikely, as Pandulpho is about to cite Seneca, who is an ancient. Antonio's decision to 'say' rather than 'sing' a dirge for Feliche is borrowed from *The Spanish Tragedy*, II.v.64–6, where Hieronimo and Isabella find the body of the murdered Horatio and Hieronimo declares, 'Come Isabel, now let us take him up, / And bear him in from out this cursed place. / I'll say his dirge, singing fits not this case.' A similar decision is made by Arviragus, *Cym.*, IV.ii.255.

74–7] From Whyttynton's *Seneca*, 'Death, exyle, mournynge, payne, and sorowe be nat tourmentes, but trybutes of thys lyfe, God suffreth no man to escape without grevaunce' (p. 65).

78–9] 'Many have carried the scars of fate with them to their graves; and death shall come to all, no man may be exempt'; cf. Whyttynton's *Seneca*: '*Sen.* Thou shalt dye. *Rea.* Nother fyrste nor last, all have gone before me, and al shal folowe me' (p. 33).

81.] i.e. the virtuous live after death.

82. *saw*] proverb.

His lazy pinion over all the air;   85
We must be stiff and steady in resolve.
Let's thus our hands, our hearts, our arms involve.

They wreathe their arms.

Pan. Now swear we by this Gordian knot of love,
By the fresh turned up mould that wraps my son,
By the dead brow of triple Hecate,   90
Ere night shall close the lids of yon bright stars
We'll sit as heavy on Piero's heart,
As Etna doth on groaning Pelorus.
Ant. Thanks, good old man. We'll cast at royal chance.
Let's think a plot; then pell-mell vengeance!   95
Exeunt, their arms wreathed.

94.] *so Bullen;* Thanks . . . man, / Weele . . . chaunce. *Q.*   95. pell-mell]
pell mell *Q.*

---

85. *pinion*] wing. '*Pinnosity*' (i.e. ? wingfulness) is one of the words
vomited by Crispinus, *Poet.*, v.iii.525. (Q only.)

87. *involve*] link together.

88. *Gordian*] that cannot be untied. An allusion to one of the feats of
Alexander the Great: 'at Gordion was a rope folded and knit with many
knots, one so wrethed within an otheir, that no man could perceyve the
maner of yt nether where the knotes began, nor wher thei ianded. Upon
theys the Countremen had a prophesie that he shuld be lord of all Asia
that could undo that endles knot . . . [Alexander tried in vain to undo it, so]
out of hand cut with his sword the cords a sondre' (Quintus Curcius, *The
Actes of The Greate Alexander*, trans. J. Brende, 1553, f. 13*v*); and *cf.*
IV.iii.70.

90. *triple Hecate*] Goddess of the underworld, with three manifestations:
as Luna (in heaven), as Diana (on earth) and as Hecate (or Proserpina) in
hell.

93. *Etna . . . Pelorus*] Pelorus, a cape in Sicily, lies 'below' (fifty miles
north of) Etna; the story is found in Ovid, *Metamorphoses*, v.346–353,
trans. A. Golding (1567): 'Bicause the Giant *Typhon* gave presumptuously
assayes / To conquer Heaven, the howgie Ile of *Trinacris* [Sicily] is layd /
Upon his limmes, by weight whereof perforce he downe is weyde. / He
strives and strugles for to rise full many a time and oft. / But on his right
hand toward *Rome Pelorus* standes aloft: / *Pachynnus* standes upon his
left: his legs with *Lilybie* / Are pressed downe: his monstrous head doth
under *Aetna* lie. / From whence he lying bolt upright with wrathfull
mouth doth spit / Out flames of fire.' (v.439–447.) Marston would, of
course, have known his Ovid in the original.

94. *cast . . . chance*] throw dice for a royal (Piero's) fate.

Act V

SCENE I.

The cornets sound for the Act.

The dumb show.

Enter at one door CASTILIO *and* FOROBOSCO *with halberts, four Pages with torches,* LUCIO *bare,* PIERO, MARIA *and* ALBERTO *talking.* ALBERTO *draws out his dagger,* MARIA *her knife, aiming to menace the Duke. Then* GALEATZO *betwixt two Senators, reading a paper to them; at which they all make semblance of loathing* PIERO *and knit their fists at him; two Ladies and* NUTRICHE. *All these go softly over the stage, whilst at the other door enters the ghost of* ANDRUGIO, *who passeth by them tossing his torch about his head in triumph. All forsake the stage, saving* ANDRUGIO, *who, speaking, begins the Act.*

Ghost of And. Venit dies, tempusque, quo reddat suis
    Animam squallentem sceleribus.
  The fist of strenuous Vengeance is clutched,

---

v.i.0.1 and 2.] *Before* Act V, Scene I. *in* Q.   1. S.H.] *Bullen; And. Q.*

---

v. This act again takes place 'within' in the palace of Piero, and each scene is artificially lit. Thus it is presumably the evening of the day which occupied Act IV.

0.8. *knit*]* clench (*O.E.D.*, *vb.* 4).

1–2.] Adapted from Seneca, *Octavia*, 629–30, 'The day has come, the time in which he pays back the foul mind for its crimes' (Hunter).

3. *strenuous*] energetic, valiant; *cf.* 'to preserve the sap of more strenuous spirits' *I Ant. & Mel.*, Ind., 34–5; this was one of the words singled out by Jonson for special condemnation: '*we list | Of strenuous venge-ance to clutch the fist*' (*Poet.*, v.ii.291–2); *cf.* also in that play II.i.13, 'most strenuously well'. It is one of the words brought up by Crispinus, v.ii.499; the word was originated by Marston.

clutched] held tightly; the word is ridiculed by Jonson, as in *Poet.*, v.iii.292, and also brought up by Crispinus, *Poet.*, v.iii.519–21. This line

And stern Vindicta tow'reth up aloft
That she may fall with a more weighty peise   5
And crush life's sap from out Piero's veins.
Now 'gins the lep'rous cores of ulcered sins
Wheel to a head; now is his fate grown mellow,
Instant to fall into the rotten jaws
Of chap-fall'n death. Now down looks providence   10
T'attend the last act of my son's revenge.
Be gracious, Observation, to our scene;
For now the plot unites his scattered limbs
Close in contracted bands. The Florence Prince
(Drawn by firm notice of the Duke's black deeds)   15
Is made a partner in conspiracy.
The States of Venice are so swoll'n in hate
Against the Duke for his accursèd deeds
(Of which they are confirmed by some odd letters
Found in dead Strotzo's study, which had passed   20
Betwixt Piero and the murd'ring slave)
That they can scarce retain from bursting forth
In plain revolt. O, now triumphs my ghost,

---

is parodied in Fletcher's *The Honest Man's Fortune* (1613): 'The strenuous fist of vengeance now is clutcht; / therefore feare nothing' (*Works*, ed. A. R. Waller, x.233). It is possible that Jonson's strictures on this expression provoked Shakespeare's remark in *Meas.*, III.ii.48–50, 'What, is there none of Pygmalion's images, newly made woman, to be had now, for putting the hand in the pocket and extracting it clutch'd?'; and *cf.* I.i.3, above.

4. *Vindicta*] Revenge; see V.iii.1.

5. *peise*] *cf.* Prol. 29 and n.

8. *wheel to a head*] i.e. circle round and swell up (like a boil or sore) to form a head.

8–10. *now . . . death*] Cf. *R3*, IV.iv.1–2, 'So now prosperity begins to mellow / And drop into the rotten mouth of death'.

9. *Instant*] immediate, ready to do so now.

10. *chap-fall'n*] the lower jaw hanging down, gaping open-mouthed; *cf.* *1 Ant. & Mel.*, IV.ii.1 'chapfall'n death'. Hamlet describes Yorick's skull as 'quite chap-fall'n' (V.i.186), and Jonson speaks of Crispinus and Demetrius as 'a couple of chap-falne curres' (*Poet.*, V.iii.341).

12. *Observation*] For Marston's habit of presenting abstract ideas in an allegorical or emblematic guise see I.i.11–12, III.i.45–6 and V.iii.59–60.

Exclaiming, 'Heaven's just; for I shall see
The scourge of murder and impiety'.   25

Exit.

SCENE II.

BALURDO *from under the stage.*

Bal. Ho! Who's above there? Ho! A murrain on all proverbs! They say hunger breaks through stone walls, but
I am as gaunt as lean-ribbed famine; yet I can burst
through no stone walls. O now, Sir Geoffrey, show thy
valour: break prison and be hanged. [*He climbs out.*]   5
 Nor shall the darkest nook of hell contain
 The discontented Sir Balurdo's ghost.
Well, I am out well; I have put off the prison to put on
the rope. O poor shotten herring, what a pickle art thou
in! O hunger, how thou domineerest in my guts! O for   10
a fat leg of ewe mutton in stewed broth, or drunken
song to feed on. I could belch rarely, for I am all wind.
O cold, cold, cold, cold, cold! O poor knight, O poor Sir

Scene II] SCENA SECVNDA *Q; not in Bullen.*   3. lean-ribbed] leane ribd
Q.   5. S.D.] *Hunter places after l. 7.*   6–7.] *so Hunter; Q prints as
prose.*

---

v.ii. 1. *murrain*] plague: cf. *Troil.*, II.i.20–1, 'A red murrain o'thy jade's
tricks!'
 2. *hunger . . . walls*] Proverb, Tilley, H.811; cf. *Cor.*, I.i.204–5, 'They
said they were an-hungry; sigh'd forth proverbs— / That hunger broke
stone walls'. The same proverb is repeated in *Eastward Ho!*, Wood
III.152.
 8–9. *put . . . rope*] because to break prison is a hanging matter.
 9. *shotten herring*] an emaciated, worthless good-for-nothing. There may
be a deliberate echo of Falstaff's ironic comment on his corpulence, *1H4*,
II.iv.124, 'I am a shotten herring'.
 pickle] D. Hoeniger points out that Balurdo's reference to 'pickled
herring' relates him to the Pickleherring clown in the plays of the English
comedians in Germany.
 10. *domineerest*]* dominatest, prevailest (*O.E.D.*, *vb.* 3).
 10–11.] See I.iii.27 n. above.

Geoffrey! Sing like an unicorn before thou dost dip thy
horn in the water of death. O cold, O sing, O cold, O   15
poor Sir Geoffrey, sing, sing!
He sings.

SCENE III.

Enter ANTONIO *and* ALBERTO *at several doors, their rapiers drawn,
in their masking attire.*

Ant. Vindicta!
Alb. Mellida!
Ant. Alberto!
Alb. Antonio!
Ant. Hath the Duke supped?   5
Alb. Yes, and triumphant revels mount aloft;
The Duke drinks deep to overflow his grief.
The court is racked to pleasure; each man strains
To feign a jocund eye. The Florentine—
Ant. Young Galeatzo?   10
Alb. Even he is mighty on our part. The States
Of Venice—

16.1.] *This ed.;* CANTAT *Q.*

Scene III] SCENA TERTIA *Q; not in Keltie, Bullen, Hunter.*

14–15. *Sing . . . death*] This is Balurdo's unnatural natural history; he is
conflating two assumptions: on the one hand it is the swan which is
reputed to sing before its death, whereas, on the other, the unicorn by
dipping its horn into water poisoned by the venom of serpents purified it
for other animals to drink. Unicorn's horn was still, in the seventeenth
century, a valued and costly ingredient in medicines, although by 1646 Sir
Thomas Browne, in *Pseudodoxia Epidemica*, expressed extreme scepticism
about the efficacy and existence of the unicorn (III.23), and expected to
hear the harmony of the Spheres as much as he anticipated hearing the
song of the dying swan (III.27).

v.iii. 0.2.] *Cf. I Ant. & Mel.*, v.ii.69.1–2, '*Enter* GALEATZO, MATZA-
GENTE, *and* BALURDO *in masquery*'.

1. Vindicta] Revenge: this is the cry of Hieronimo, *Spanish Tragedy*,
III.xiii.1, '*Vindicta mihi.*' The cry is parodied by Fletcher in *The Fair Maid
of the Inn*, 1626 (*Works*, ed. A. R. Waller, IX.174), the clown crying,
'*Vindicta, Vindicta*,' for his broken pate. See also v.i.4.

8. *racked*] stretched, strained.

Enter PANDULPHO *running, in masking attire.*

Pan. Like high-swoll'n floods, drive down the muddy dams
       Of pent allegiance! O, my lusty bloods,
       Heaven sits clapping of our enterprise.   15
       I have been labouring general favour firm,
       And I do find the citizens grown sick
       With swallowing the bloody crudities
       Of black Piero's acts; they fain would cast
       And vomit him from off their government.   20
       Now is the plot of mischief ripped wide ope:
       Letters are found 'twixt Strotzo and the Duke
       So clear apparent, yet more firmly strong
       By suiting circumstance, that as I walked
       Muffled, to eavesdrop speech, I might observe   25
       The graver statesmen whispering fearfully.
       Here one gives nods and hums what he would speak;
       The rumour's got 'mong troop of citizens
       Making loud murmur with confusèd din:
       One shakes his head and sighs, 'O ill-used power!'   30
       Another frets and sets his grinding teeth
       Foaming with rage, and swears, 'This must not be!':
       Here one complots and on a sudden starts,
       And cries, 'O monstrous, O deep villainy!'.
       All knit their nerves and from beneath swoll'n brows   35
       Appears a gloating eye of much mislike;
       Whilst swart Piero's lips reek steam of wine,
       Swallows lust-thoughts, devours all pleasing hopes
       With strong imagination of—what not?

25. eavesdrop] eves-drop *Q*.   30. ill-used] illus'd *Q*.

---

14. *pent*]* closely confined (*O.E.D.*, *ppl. a.* 1).
16.] i.e. I have been strongly endeavouring to rouse up public opinion.
18. *crudities*] undigested pieces of food.
19. *cast*] throw up from within.
25. *eavesdrop*]* listen secretly (to); cf. *Fawn*, III.i.206, 'look that nobody
eavesdrop us'.
33. *complots*] conspires.

O, now, *Vindicta*! that's the word we have: 40
A royal vengeance, or a royal grave.

Ant. *Vindicta!*

Bal. [*Prone.*] I am a-cold.

Pan.   Who's there? Sir Geoffrey?

Bal. A poor knight, God wot; the nose of my knighthood is
bitten off with cold. O poor Sir Geoffrey, cold, cold!

Pan. What chance of fortune hath tripped up his heels   45
And laid him in the kennel? Ha!

Alb. I will discourse it all. Poor honest soul,
Hadst thou a beaver to clasp up thy face
Thou shouldst associate us in masquery
And see revenge.   50

Bal. Nay, and you talk of revenge, my stomach's up, for I
am most tyrannically hungry. A beaver? I have a head-
piece, a skull, a brain of proof, I warrant ye.

Alb. Slink to my chamber then and tire thee.

Bal. Is there a fire?

Alb.   Yes.   55

Bal. Is there a fat leg of ewe mutton?

Alb.   Yes.

Bal. And a clean shirt?

Alb.   Yes.

Bal. Then am I for you, most pathetically and unvulgarly, la!

                                        Exit.

Ant. Resolved hearts, time curtails night, Opportunity
shakes us his foretop. Steel your thoughts, sharp your   60

---

42. *Vindicta!* . . . Geoffrey?] *so this ed.; three lines* Q. [*Prone.*] *This ed.;*
[*From beneath the stage.*] *Bullen.* a-cold] acolde Q.   43. my] *1633;* thy Q.
55–7. Is . . . Yes. / Is . . . Yes. / And . . . Yes.] *so this ed.; six lines* Q.

---

40. *word*] slogan.
46. *kennel*] gutter.
48. *beaver*] helmet, face guard.
51. *stomach*] i.e. hunger and anger.
53. *a brain of proof*] an impenetrable brain (i.e. Balurdo ironically
reveals his stupidity while asserting his courage); see II.ii.19 n.
54. *tire*] attire.
59–60. *Opportunity . . . foretop*] In G. Wither's *A Collection of Emblemes,*

resolve, embolden your spirit, grasp your swords,
alarum mischief, and with an undaunted brow out-
scout the grim opposition of most menacing peril.

[*Sounds of revelry within.*]

Hark! Here proud pomp shoots mounting triumph up,
Borne in loud accents to the front of Jove.   65
Pan. O now, he that wants soul to kill a slave,
    Let him die slave and rot in peasant's grave.
Ant. [*To* ALBERTO] Give me thy hand, [*To* PANDULPHO]
    and thine, most noble heart;
    Thus will we live and, but thus, never part.

                    Exeunt twined together.

SCENE IV.
Cornets sound a sennet.

Enter CASTILIO *and* FOROBOSCO, *two Pages with torches*, LUCIO
bare, PIERO *and* MARIA, GALEATZO, *two Senators and* NUTRICHE.

Pie. *To* MARIA
    Sit close unto my breast, heart of my love;
    Advance thy drooping eyes; thy son is drowned
    (Rich happiness that such a son is drowned!),
    Thy husband's dead. Life of my joys, most blessed,
    In that the sapless log that pressed thy bed   5
    With an unpleasing weight, being lifted hence,

62–3. out-scout] out scout *Q.*   64. Hark! Here proud] *Bullen subst.*;
Harke here, proud *Q;* Hark, hear! Proud *Hunter.*

Scene IV] SCENA QVARTA *Q; Scene II Bullen; Scene III Keltie, Hunter.*
0.1.] *so Hunter; Q prints at V.iii.65.1.*   0.4. *To* MARIA] *This ed.; Piero to
Maria Q.*   2.] *so Bullen;* Aduance . . . eyes / Thy . . . drownde *Q.*

Ancient and Moderne (1635) Book I, p. 4, Occasion or Opportunity is
depicted with a flowing forelock (for the quick to seize).

    62. *out-scout*] outmanoeuvre.
    64. *Here*] Hunter may be right in reading 'hear!', for Q is ambiguous.
    v.iv. 2. *Advance*] raise.

Even I, Piero, live to warm his place.
I tell you, lady, had you viewed us both
With an unpartial eye when first we wooed
Your maiden beauties, I had borne the prize.   10
'Tis firm I had; for, fair, I ha' done that—
Mar. [*Aside*] Murder!
Pie. Which he would quake to have adventured.
Thou know'st I have—
Mar. [*Aside*] Murdered my husband.   15
Pie. Borne out the shock of war, and done, what not,
That valour durst. Dost love me, fairest? Say!
Mar. As I do hate my son, I love thy soul.
Pie. Why then, Io to Hymen! Mount a lofty note,
Fill red-cheeked Bacchus, let Lyaeus float   20
In burnished goblets! Force the plump-lipped god
Skip light lavoltas in your full-sapped veins!   [*Takes goblet.*]
'Tis well, brim-full. Even I have glut of blood.
Let quaff carouse: I drink this Bordeaux wine
Unto the health of dead Andrugio,   25
Feliche, Strotzo, and Antonio's ghosts.

20. red-cheeked] red cheekt *Q.*   21. plump-lipped] plump lipt *Q.*
22. full-sapped] full sapt *Q.*   23. brim-full] brim full *Q.*

---

11. *firm*] certain.
19. *Io to Hymen !*] Praise the wedding god.
20. *Lyaeus*] An epithet applied to Bacchus, meaning 'the care-dispeller'.
22. *lavoltas*] A lively dance for two persons, consisting a good deal in high and active bounds; cf. Chapman, *May Day* (1602), IV.i.14–15, 'Fill red-cheek'd Bacchus, let the Bourdeaux grape / Skip like la voltas in their swelling veins.' Chapman may be parodying Marston here, as he puts the words of Piero into the mouth of the swaggering cheater Quintiliano. The dance is described by Sir John Davies, *Orchestra* (1596), Stanza 70: 'Yet is there one, the most delightful kind, / A lofty jumping, or a leaping round, / When arm in arm two dancers are entwin'd, / And whirl themselves with strict embracements bound, / And still their feet an anapest do sound; / An anapest is all their music's song, / When first two feet are short and third is long'.
full-sapped] having plenty of sap or spirit.
24. *Let quaff carouse*] Let us drink toasts; cf. *Shr.*, I.ii.273, 'quaff carouses to our mistress' health'.

[*Aside*] Would I had some poison to infuse it with,
That, having done this honour to the dead,
I might send one to give them notice on't!
I would endear my favour to the full.　　　　　　　30
[*To Page*] Boy, sing aloud, make heaven's vault to ring
With thy breath's strength. I drink. Now loudly sing.
　　　　　　　　He sings.

SCENE V.
The song ended, the cornets sound a sennet.
Enter ANTONIO, PANDULPHO, *and* ALBERTO *in maskery,*
BALURDO *and a torch-bearer.*

Pie. Call Julio hither; where's the little soul?
　　I saw him not today. Here's sport alone
　　For him, i'faith; for babes and fools, I know,
　　Relish not substance but applaud the show.
Gal. [*Aside*] *to the conspirators as they stand in rank for the*
　　measure.
　　To ANTONIO
　　All blessèd fortune crown your brave attempt.　　　5
　　To PANDULPHO
　　I have a troop to second your attempt.

32.1.] *This ed.;* CANTAT *Q; A Song Bullen.*
Scene V] SCENA QVINTA *Q; not in Keltie, Bullen, Hunter.*　　0.1. *The ...*
sennet] *precedes* Scene V *in Q.*

30.] i.e. I would in that case enjoy the entire favour of the dead.
　v.v. The action of this scene and scene vi is examined in detail in the Introduction, p. 28.
　2. *alone*] especially: *cf. MND.* III.ii.118–19, 'Then will two at once woo one: / That must needs be sport alone'.
　4.2. measure] A stately and formal dance of elegance, serenity and gravity: described by Sir John Davies, *Orchestra,* Stanza 65, 'But after these [round dances], as men more civil grew / He [Love] did more grave and solemn measures fame; / With such fair order and proportion true / And correspondence every way the same / That no fault-finding eye did ever blame; / For every eye was moved at the sight / With sober wond'ring and with sweet delight'.

To ALBERTO
The Venice States join hearts unto your hands.

Pie. By the delights in contemplation
Of coming joys, 'tis magnificent.
You grace my marriage eve with sumptuous pomp.   10
Sound still, loud music. O, your breath gives grace
To curious feet that in proud measure pace.

Ant. [*Aside*] Mother, is Julio's body—

Mar. [*Aside*] Speak not, doubt not; all is above all hope.

Ant. [*Aside*] Then will I dance and whirl about the air: 15
Methinks I am all soul, all heart, all spirit.
Now murder shall receive his ample merit.

The Measure.
While the measure is dancing, ANDRUGIO'S *ghost is
placed betwixt the music houses.*

Pie. Bring hither suckets, candied delicates.
We'll taste some sweetmeats, gallants, ere we sleep.

Ant. [*Aside*] We'll cook your sweetmeats, gallants, with tart   20
sour sauce!

Ghost of And. [*Aside*]
Here will I sit, spectator of revenge,
And glad my ghost in anguish of my foe.

The maskers whisper with PIERO.

Pie. Marry, and shall; i'faith I were too rude
If I gainsaid so civil fashion.   25
[*To the Courtiers and Attendants*]
The maskers pray you to forbear the room
Till they have banqueted. Let it be so;

22. S.H.] *Bullen; And. Q.*

---

12. *curious*] skilful.
17.3. music houses] See Introduction, pp. 27–8.
18. *suckets*] sweetmeats, candied fruit.
candied] preserved with sugar (*O.E.D.*, *ppl. a.* 1).
25. *gainsaid*] opposed.

No man presume to visit them, on death.   [*Exeunt Courtiers*
       The maskers whisper again.   *and Attendants.*]
Only my self? O, why, with all my heart.
I'll fill your consort; here Piero sits.   30
Come on, unmask; let's fall to.

    The conspirators [unmask and] bind PIERO.

Ant. Murder and torture; no prayers, no entreats.
Pan. We'll spoil your oratory. Out with his tongue!

    [*They*] *pluck out his tongue and triumph over him.*

Ant. I have't, Pandulpho; the veins panting bleed,
    Trickling fresh gore about my fist. Bind fast! So, so.   35
Ghost of And. Blest be thy hand. I taste the joys of heaven,
    Viewing my son triumph in his black blood.
Bal. Down to the dungeon with him; I'll dungeon with
    him; I'll fool you! Sir Geoffrey will be Sir Geoffrey. I'll
    tickle you!
Ant. Behold, black dog! [*Holding up* PIERO'S *tongue.*]
Pan.   Grinn'st thou, thou snurling cur?   40
Alb. Eat thy black liver!
Ant.   To thine anguish see
    A fool triumphant in thy misery.
    Vex him, Balurdo.
Pan. He weeps! Now do I glorify my hands.
    I had no vengeance if I had no tears.   45

31.1, 33.1.] *This ed.; The conspirators binde Piero, pluck out his tongue, and
tryumph ouer him at 31.1 in Q.*
40–1. Behold . . . our? / Eat . . . see] *so Hunter; four lines Q.*

---

    30. *consort*] company.
    33.1.] The same fate befell Shakespeare's Lavinia, *Tit.*, II.iv, and in
The Spanish Tragedy Hieronimo bit out his own tongue (IV.iv.191.1).
    44–5. *Now . . . tears*] From Seneca, *Thyestes*, 1096–8: '*Atreus.* Nunc
meas laudo manus, / nunc parta vera est palma. perdideram scelus, / Nisi
sic doleres.' (Now do I praise my handiwork, now is the true palm won. I
had wasted my crime, didst thou not suffer thus.)

Ant. [*Points to the table of sweetmeats.*]
    Fall to, good Duke. O these are worthless cates.
    You have no stomach to them. Look, look here:
    Here lies a dish to feast thy father's gorge.
    Here's flesh and blood which I am sure thou lovest.
    [*Uncovering the dish that contains* JULIO'S *limbs*]

PIERO *seems to condole his son.*

Pan. Was he thy flesh, thy son, thy dearest son?   50
Ant. So was Andrugio my dearest father.
Pan. So was Feliche my dearest son.

Enter MARIA.

Mar. So was Andrugio my dearest husband.
Ant. My father found no pity in thy blood.
Pan. Remorse was banished when thou slew'st my son.   55
Mar. When thou empoisonèd'st my loving lord,
    Exiled was piety.
Ant. Now, therefore, pity, piety, remorse,
    Be aliens to our thoughts; grim fire-eyed rage
    Possess us wholly.   60
Pan. Thy son? True; and which is my most joy,
    I hope no bastard but thy very blood,
    Thy true-begotten, most legitimate
    And lovèd issue: there's the comfort on't!

49.1.] *Bullen.*   63. true-begotten] true begotten *Q.*

---

46. *cates*] provisions.
49.] *Cf.* Ovid, *Met.*, VI; King Tereus' rape and mutilation of Philomela
are discovered by his wife, Procne, sister to Philomela; the two women
murder Tereus' son Itys: 'And while some life and soule was in his
members yit, / In Gobbits they them rent: whereof were some in Pipkin's
boyld, / And other some on hissing spits against the fire were broyld: /
And with the gellied blood of him was all the chamber soyld. / To this
same banket *Progne* bade hir husband, knowing nought' (813–18, trans.
Golding). A similar situation occurs in *Tit.*, V.iii.

Ant. Scum of the mud of hell!
Alb.   Slime of all filth!   65
Mar. Thou most detested toad.
Bal. Thou most retort and obtuse rascal!
Ant. Thus charge we death at thee. Remember hell;
        And let the howling murmurs of black spirits,
        The horrid torments of the damnèd ghosts,   70
        Affright thy soul as it descendeth down
        Into the entrails of the ugly deep.
Pan. Sa, sa; no, let him die and die, and still be dying.

        They offer to run all at PIERO *and on a sudden stop.*

        And yet not die, till he hath died and died
        Ten thousand deaths in agony of heart.   75
Ant. Now, pell-mell! Thus the hand of heaven chokes
        The throat of murder. This for my father's blood!
                                            He stabs PIERO
Pan. This for my son! [*Stabs him.*]
Alb.   This for them all!   [*Stabs him.*]
        And this, and this; sink to the heart of hell!

        They run all at PIERO *with their rapiers.*

Pan. Murder for murder, blood for blood doth yell.   80
Ghost of And. 'Tis done, and now my soul shall sleep in rest.
        Sons that revenge their father's blood are blest.
                        The curtains being drawn, exit ANDRUGIO.

---

65. Scum . . . filth!] *so this ed.; two lines* Q.   76. pell-mell] pel mell Q.
78. This . . . all!] *so this ed.; two lines* Q.   81. S.H.] *Bullen; Andr.* Q.

---

66. *Thou . . . toad*] In *R3*, IV.iv.145, the Duchess of York addresses
Richard as 'Thou toad, thou toad', and in Middleton and Rowley's *The
Changeling*, II.i.58, Beatrice calls De Flores a 'standing toad-pool'.
73. *Sa, sa*] 'hunting call, to urge forward the hounds' (Hunter).

SCENE VI.

Enter GALEATZO, *two Senators,* LUCIO, FOROBOSCO, CASTILIO,
and Ladies.

1st. Sen. Whose hand presents this gory spectacle ?
Ant. Mine.
Pan.   No! Mine.
Alb.   No! Mine.
Ant. I will not lose the glory of the deed,
         Were all the tortures of the deepest hell
         Fixed to my limbs. I pierced the monster's heart   5
         With an undaunted hand.
Pan. By yon bright-spangled front of heaven, 'twas I;
         'Twas I sluiced out his life-blood.
Alb. Tush, to say truth, 'twas all.
2nd. Sen. Blest be you all, and may your honours live   10
         Religiously held sacred, even for ever and ever.
Gal. *To* ANTONIO Thou art another Hercules to us
         In ridding huge pollution from our state.
1st. Sen. Antonio, belief is fortified
         With most invincible approvements of much wrong   15
         By this Piero to thee. We have found
         Beadrolls of mischief, plots of villainy,
         Laid 'twixt the Duke and Strotzo; which we found
         Too firmly acted.
2nd. Sen.   Alas, poor orphan !
Ant. Poor ?   20

Scene VI] SCENA SEXTA *Q;* not in *Keltie, Bullen, Hunter.*   2. Mine . . .
Mine] *so this ed.; three lines Q.*   3. lose] *1633;* loose *Q.*   7. bright-
spangled] bright spangled *Q.*   8. life-blood] life bloode *Q.*   19. Two
. . . orphan!] *so Hunter; two lines Q.*   20–2. Poor ? / Standing . . . Belzebub ?
/ Having . . . poor ?] *so Bullen;* Poor . . . Belzebub ? / Having . . . poore ? *Q.*

v.vi. 11. *for . . . ever*] K. Schoonover points out that this is probably
designed to recall the repetitive liturgical phrase 'for ever and ever. Amen.'
     12. *Hercules*] Hercules' fifth labour was to clean the dung from the
Augeian stables; he did so by diverting the rivers Alpheius and Peneius.
     15. *approvements*]* evidence, proofs.
     17. *beadrolls*] a catalogue, a long series.
     19. *firmly acted*] resolutely performed.

Standing triumphant over Belzebub ?
Having large interest for blood, and yet deemed poor ?

1st. Sen. What satisfaction outward pomp can yield,
Or chiefest fortunes of the Venice state,
Claim freely. You are well-seasoned props   25
And will not warp or lean to either part:
'Calamity gives man a steady heart'.

Ant. We are amazed at your benignity;
But other vows constrain another course.

Pan. We know the world, and did we know no more   30
We would not live to know; but since constraint
Of holy bands forceth us keep this lodge
Of dirt's corruption till dread power calls
Our souls' appearance, we will live enclosed
In holy verge of some religious order,   35
Most constant votaries.

The curtains are drawn; PIERO *departeth.*

Ant. First let's cleanse our hands,
Purge hearts of hatred and entomb my love;
Over whose hearse I'll weep away my brain
In true affection's tears.   40
For her sake here I vow a virgin bed:

25. well-seasoned] well seasoned *Q.*

---

22. *interest for blood*] i.e. he has spilt far more of the blood of his
enemies than he has lost of his own.

24. *chiefest fortunes*] highest positions.

25. *well-seasoned*] matured by experience (*O.E.D., ppl. a.* 3).

26. *either part*] either of the two sides in a dispute.

27.] Proverb; Tilley, c.15a, 'Calamity is the touchstone of a brave mind';
the idea is Senecan: *Oedipus,* 386, 'solent suprema facere securos mala'
(Extremest ills are wont to make men calm).

28.] Antonio's surprise is caused by the fact that the Senators make no
comment on his blood guilt; he, however, is aware of the need for penance
even if they are not—see Introduction, pp. 38–9.

30–1. *and . . . know*] i.e. if we had no knowledge beyond that of worldly
things we could not bear to continue living.

31–4. *but . . . appearance*] i.e. the Christian prohibition of suicide.

33. *dirt's corruption*] mortal clay.

34. *appearance*] i.e. after death for judgement.

35. *verge*]* the pale or limit of a (religious) community (*O.E.D., sb.*[1] 12.*b*).

She lives in me, with her my love is dead.
2nd. Sen. We will attend her mournful exequies;
    Conduct you to your calm sequestered life,
    And then—   45
Mar. Leave us to meditate on misery,
    To sad our thought with contemplation
    Of past calamities. If any ask
    Where lives the widow of the poisoned lord,
    Where lies the orphan of a murdered father,   50
    Where lies the father of a butchered son,
    Where lives all woe, conduct him to us three,
    The downcast ruins of calamity.
Ant. Sound doleful tunes, a solemn hymn advance,
    To close the last act of my vengeance;   55
    And when the subject of your passion's spent,
    Sing 'Mellida is dead', all hearts will relent
    In sad condolement at that heavy sound;
    Never more woe in lesser plot was found.
    And, O, if ever time create a muse   60
    That to th' immortal fame of virgin faith
    Dares once engage his pen to write her death,
    Presenting it in some black tragedy,
    May it prove gracious, may his style be decked
    With freshest blooms of purest elegance;   65
    May it have gentle presence, and the scenes sucked up
    By calm attention of choice audience;
    And when the closing Epilogue appears,
    Instead of claps, may it obtain but tears.
                 They sing.   *Exeunt all.*

        The End of Antonio's Revenge.

---

54. S.H.] *Bullen; And.* Q.   69.1. *They Sing*] *This ed.;* CANTANT Q.
Exeunt all] *This ed.; Exeunt omnes* Q.   69.2.] *This ed.; Antonij vindictae*
/ FINIS Q.

58. *condolement*]* lamentation.
59. *plot*] area, and also 'plot' of the play.
66. *gentle presence*] i.e. in the company of gentlemen and ladies and in a
graceful setting.

Publisher's preface to the 1633 edition, first issue

To the Right Honourable, the Lady Elizabeth Carie, Viscountesse Fawkland.

Many opprobies and aspersions have not long since been cast upon Playes in generall, and it were requisite and expedient that they were vindicated from them; But I referre that taske to those whose leasure is greater, and Learning more transcendent. Yet for my part I cannot perceive wherein they should appeare so vile and abhominable, that they should bee so vehemently inveighed against; Is it because they are Playes? The name it seems somewhat offends them, whereas if they were styled Workes, they might have their Approbation also. I hope that I have now somewhat pacified that precise Sect, by reducing all our Authors severall Playes into one Volume, and so stiled them *The Works of Mr.* JOHN MARSTON: who was not inferiour unto any in this kinde of Writing, in those dayes when these were penned, and I am perswaded equall unto the best Poets of our times. If the lines bee not answerable to my Encomium of him, yet herein beare with him, because they were his *Iuvenilia*, and youthfull Recreations; Howsoever hee is free from all obscene speeches, which is the chiefe cause that makes Playes to bee so odious unto most men. Hee abhorres such Writers, and their Workes, and hath professed himselfe an enemie to all such as stuffe their Scenes with ribaldry, and lard their lines with scurrilous taunts and jests: so that whatsoever even in the Spring of his yeeres hee hath presented upon the private and publike Theatre, now in his Autumne, and declining age hee need not bee ashamed of; and were it not that hee is so farre distant from this place, hee would have beene more carefull in revising the former Impressions, and more circumspect about this, then I can. In his absence, Noble Lady, I have been imboldened to present these Workes unto your Honours view, and the rather, because your Honour is well acquainted with the Muses; In briefe, Fame hath given out, that your Honour is the

Mirror of your sex, the admiration, not onely of this Iland, but of all adjacent Countries and Dominions, which are acquainted with your rare Vertues, and Endowments: If your Honour shall vouchsafe to accept this Worke, I with my Booke am ready prest and bound to be

Your truly devoted,
WILLIAM SHEARES.

Marston's use of words in *Antonio's Revenge*

This appendix supplies the data upon which the word usage calculations on p. 20 of the Introduction are based, and replaces the index to annotations found in most other Revels volumes. Words listed with an asterisk are those which are either not recorded in *O.E.D.* in the sense they bear in *Antonio's Revenge*, or which are listed but with examples only from texts of a later date. All words glossed in the commentary are included, but longer phrases which are paraphrased there are often not included. The words are cited in this appendix in the spelling of the quarto text of 1602.

In compiling this appendix two difficult problems have had to be faced. Quite often Marston uses a word, familiar in his day, in a fresh metaphorical sense, and as *O.E.D.* does not include such meanings in its definitions (except for the occasional figurative listing) they have not been included here. The same policy has been applied to a number of compounds, like 'plump-lipped', because the editors of *O.E.D.* included only a limited number of these. A few compounds, however, which seem to me to have probably been first coined by Marston have been included. Some of the words listed here as first used by Marston may, of course, be antedated by other literary usages unknown to *O.E.D.*

The references to the plays of Shakespeare are derived from J. Bartlett's *Concordance* (1953) and to the works of Spenser from the C. G. Osgood *Concordance* (Gloucester, Mass., 1963). In both cases only one example is cited (although there are often several available). References given in square brackets indicate a usage which is only similar, but closely so, to Marston's. As there is, to date, no reliable concordance to Jonson, the listings in the fourth column do not pretend to be exhaustive: those from *Catiline* and *Sejanus* are derived from L. C. Stagg, *Index to the Figurative Language of Ben Jonson's Tragedies* (Virginia, 1967).

MARSTON	SHAKESPEARE	SPENSER	JONSON
Abortiue I.ii.20	2H6 IV.i.60		
Abstract★ II.i.65			
Acclamations II.v.17	Cor. I.ix.51	S.C. May 164	
Accordance III.iii.16			
Act I.v.104	[AYL II.vii.143]		
Aduance V.iv.2	Tp. I.ii.408		
Affect I.ii.52	LLL. I.ii.172	S.C. Nov. 145	
Affectes I.v.38	LLL. I.i.152	F.Q. VI.i.45.2	B.F. IV.iii.3
Affied II.iii.50	Shr.IV.iv.49	F.Q. IV.viii.53.1	
Alone V.v.2	MND. III.iii.119		
Antic IV.v.72	Ham. v.ii.352		
Apish I.v.80	John V.ii.131	Hub. 731	[B.F. III.vi.52]
Apocrypha IV.i.22			Alc. I.iii.41
Apparent IV.iii.10	Meas. IV.ii.144	Ded. Son. XI.8	
Approuemēts★ V.vi.15			
Arte IV.i.20	AYL. III.ii.31	Colin 702	
Aspectes Prol. 6	R2 I.iii.127	F.Q. III.vi.12.2	Poet., To the Reader, 224
Assur'd I.ii.27	Err. III.ii.145	F.Q. II.iv.23.9	
Astonning★ III.ii.25		[F.Q. V.vii.54.5]	
Atonement I.iii.110	R3 I.iii.36	F.Q. V.viii.21.8	
Babl'd★ IV.i.19			
Balkes IV.v.35	Lucr. 696	F.Q. III.ii.12.3	Poet. I.ii.217
Bankrout II.iv.22	Err. IV.ii.58		
Beadroles V.vi.17		F.Q. IV.ii.32.9	
Beaking II.iii.52			

MARSTON	SHAKESPEARE	SPENSER	JONSON
Cheers I.iii.105	Tp. I.i.2	F.Q. VI Pr. I.9	
Chide I.v.88	Tp. I.ii.476	F.Q. IV.xii.23.2	[Cat. I.81]
Choice IV.ii.13	2H4 I.iii.11	Ruins/Time 333	
Choke I.i.74	Meas. V.i.427	F.Q. I.iii.8.1	[Cat. IV.417]
Chub-fac't IV.i.42			
Clap II.i.9	Caes. I.ii.261	[F.Q. III.x.12.9]	
Clapper II.ii.50	Ado III.ii.13		
Clawe I.i.46	Ado I.iii.13		
Cleaue IV.iii.70	Meas. III.i.63	F.Q. V.i.10.7	
Clipt I.i.63	Cym. V.v.451	F.Q. III.xii.45 or I	
Close II.iii.68	H5 I.ii.182		
Cloucht I.i.3	Cor. III.iii.17	[F.Q. III.x.20.2]	Poet. v.iii.519–22 (parody)
Clumzie Prol. I			Poet. v.iii.485–6 (parody)
Cluttered I.v.60			
Coate IV.iii.104			
Cockeall* III.iv.6			
Colour de Roy I.iii.14			
Complots v.iii.33	R2 I.iii.189	[F.Q. V.viii.25.3]	
Condolement* v.vi.58	Ham. I.ii.93		
Confluence IV.iii.I	Tim. I.i.42		Poet. v.ii.40
Congruence Prol. 8			
Conscious* I.i.76			
Consort Prol. 26	Rom. III.i.49	F.Q. II.v.31.8	
Conuerse IV.iii.176	1H6 II.i.25		Poet. v.iii.287–8 (parody)
Coope* I.i.11	[John II.i.25]	[S.C. Oct. 72]	

Corb'd* II.ii.86			
Courts I.ii.10			
Coyle I.v.89	Tim. I.ii.236	[F.Q. II.ix.2.5]	[Cat. I.4II], B.F. I.iv.34
Crackling I.ii.53			
Craggie IV.iii.70			
Cropt I.i.26	Ant. II.ii.233	F.Q. IV.vii.25.6	
Crudities* II.v.31			
Cunger II.i.30	2H4 II.iv.266	Ruins/Rome XXIX.4	
Curious V.v.12	Cym. V.v.361	[Hymn/Beauty 137]	
Damps* I.iii.74	Ant. IV.ix.13		[Cat. III.460]
Danke Prol. I	Caes. II.i.263		
Dead I.i.3	[2H4 I.i.72]		
Decocting* IV.iii.37	[2H6 III.i.123]	F.Q. VI.xi.42.2]	
Defame II.iii.19			
Deserless* I.v.69		F.Q. IV.v.17.5	
Deuice I.iii.27	1H6 I.ii.41		
Deuoyer Prol. 9		S.C. Sept. 227	
Dingd IV.iii.83			
Disease II.ii.103	Cor. I.iii.117	S.C. July 124	
Dominer'st* V.iii.10	[Shr. III.ii.226]		Cyn. Rev. V.iv.326 (? parody)
Dropsie IV.iii.58	Tp. IV.i.230	F.Q. I.iv.23.7	
Elate IV.i.2			
Empoyson'd (Impoyson'd)* III.v.10	Cor. V.vi.11		[Alc. V.v.9], [Cat. I.550]
Enchanting (Inchanting)* IV.ii.3	Ant. I.ii.132	[Astrophel 46]	

MARSTON	SHAKESPEARE	SPENSER	JONSON
Enfolds (Infolds)* II.i.1	Tit. I.i.252	[F.Q. I.x.13.4]	Cyn. Rev. V.iv.141 (parody)
Ensigne I.iii.131	R3 III.vii.225	[F.Q. VI.iii.38.5]	
Entreats I.ii.4	[R3 v.iii.221]		
Eves-drop* v.iii.25	Tp. I.ii.99		
Exact I.v.103	1H6 III.ii.133		
Exequies IV.iii.196	R3 I.ii.166		Poet. III.iii.25 (parody)
Exhale I.iii.83	R3 III.vii.192		
Expostulate IV.iv.3	Ham. II.i.38		
Fetch II.ii.33			
Flagge* III.iii.29			
Flare III.ii.6	Wiv. IV.vi.42	[F.Q. v.xii.38.8]	
Fleamie II.iii.54			
Fleering I.i.61	LLL. v.ii.109	[Hub. 714]	
Fleet III.ii.60	Mer. V. III.ii.108	Colin 286	Poet. v.iii.288 (parody)
Fluent* Prol. 2	[H5 III.vii.36]		
Fluxe IV.iii.3	AYL. II.i.52		
Fomie II.iii.54	[Tw.N. v.i.81]		
Fresh pauncht I.iii.43			
Froathy II.ii.83	1H4 III.i.14	[F.Q. I.xi.23.3]	
Front I.ii.19		Gnat 686	
Fulgor I.ii.8			
Full sapt v.iv.22			
Fume I.v.89	Rom. I.i.196	Colin 608	Cyn. Rev. I.iii.44 (? parody)
Fut I.i.80	2H4 I.i.91	F.Q. VI.ii.18.9	
Gainesaide v.v.25			

Galleasse IV.ii.50		Shr. II.i.381	B.F. II.ii.65
Galled I.v.45	[F.Q. IV.v.31.8]	Ham. III.ii.253	
Gaudes I.ii.58		MND. IV.i.172	
Gellied* I.iii.74	[F.Q. III.iv.40.6]		Poet. v.iii.382 (parody)
Girde II.v.26	S.C. April 134	Sonn. XII.7	
Girne I.iii.12	F.Q. v.xii.15.8	John III.iv.34	
Glib* I.ii.17	[F.Q. IV.viii.12.6]	Lr. I.i.227	
Glimmering I.ii.23		MND. III.ii.61	
Gloss'd* I.v.39			
Great* I.iii.76	Colin 854	[Tim. IV.iii.189]	
Gripe I.v.85	F.Q. II.vii.27.7	H8 v.iii.100	
Ground I.i.21	F.Q. VI.i.1.5	Lr. II.iv.146	
Habit IV.i.4	Hub. 84	Tw.N. v.i.396	
Hale I.i.78	F.Q. VI.viii.6.7	Tw.N. III.ii.64	
Halfe-clamd* III.iii.44			
Half-rot III.i.10			
Hell-straid (or strain'd) III.ii.70			Poet. I.ii.185 (? parody)
High-lone IV.iv.9			
High-nol'd IV.iii.48			
Honey* I.i.83	[Colin 596]	[Troil. v.ii.18]	
Hoope IV.i.66		Wint. IV.iv.450	
Howling* I.i.7	[F.Q. I.ii.23.2]	Oth. II.i.68	
Hug* II.i.10			
Humours I.v.98	F.Q. II.iii.9.8	Wiv. III.iii.181	Poet. III.i.6
Husht I.i.71			

MARSTON	SHAKESPEARE	SPENSER	JONSON
Hymniall* III.v.i	Meas. II.iv.11	Gnat 8	B.F. IV.i.52
Idle III.ii.30			
Ill relisht II.iii.4			
Illustrate IV.iii.7	LLL. v.i.128		
Imbraid (Embraid) I.iv.8			
Imperiall IV.ii.2	MND. II.i.163	F.Q. II.v.10.1	
Importunate* II.v.22	Ham. IV.v.2		
Impulsive* II.v.18			
Inamorate* I.i.103	Ham. I.iv.42		Poet. III.i.31 (parody of vb.)
Incestuous I.iv.17			
Inchac't (Enchased) IV.iii.171			
Incubus* I.i.90	2H6 I.ii.8	S.C. Aug. 27	Poet. v.iii.282 (parody)
Indeere (Endear) II.i.48	[John IV.ii.228]	Hymn/Love 274	Poet. III.iv.80 (parody)
Innating* IV.i.46			
Instant V.i.9	Tim. III.ii.41	F.Q. VI.xi.9.7	
Intellect* III.i.18	[R2 V.i.28]		
Intimate* II.i.48	[Tw.N. II.v.94]		
Inuolue IV.v.87			
Iubile (Jubile) I.iii.109			
Iuyceles (Juiceles)* Pro			
Jack I.v.49	R3 I.iii.53		
Jades (Iades) I.v.72	Gent. III.i.277	F.Q. VI.vii.40.7	B.F. I.i.17
Jawne (Iawne)* II.ii.72			
Kennell v.iii.46	Shr. IV.iii.98		

Knit* v.i.0.8	[John III.i.226]		
Knurly* IV.iii.72			
Lackie Prol. 28	[Ant. I.iv.46]	F.Q. VI.ii.15.5	
Lagd* I.i.80	[R2 I.iii.214]	[F.Q. VI.ii.10.6]	
Lampe III.i.6	[Ant. I.iv.5]		[Sej. II.452]
Lawne II.iii.12	Oth. IV.iii.73		
Leapred I.v.83			
Legge III.iv.19	All's W. II.iii.10		
Lethargy IV.ii.18	Tw.N. I.v.132		
Lifen* II.v.17			
Licorish II.ii.36			
Light I.ii.61	Meas. V.i.280	S.C. June 103	
List II.ii.80	Ham. I. v.177	S.C. May 164	Poet. V.iii.291 (parody)
Log-like* I.v.37			
Maine (Maim) I.iv.20	R2 I.iii.156		
Malepert IV.iii.119	R3 I.iii.255		
Mangle III.iii.58	Rom. III.iii.51		
Marrish II.iii.55		[Hymn/Love 143]	
Mart* IV.iii.177	[Ham. I.i.74]	[S.C. Sept. 37]	
Massy Prol. 30	Ham. III.iii.17	F.Q. V.xi.21.8	Alc. III.ii.45
Maugre II.ii.85	Tw.N. III.i.163	Hub. 816	
Mawe IV.v.31	[Rom. V.iii.45]	[F.Q. I.iv.30.5]	
Mimic* I.v.78	[MND. III.ii.19]	[Tears/Muses 207]	
Monopoly IV.ii.53	Lr. I.iv.167		
Morally IV.i.30			
Motion IV.i.63	Wiv. I.i.55		

MARSTON	SHAKESPEARE	SPENSER	JONSON
Muffe IV.iii.130			
Murre III.iv.42			
Murren V.ii.1	*Troil.* II.i.20	*F.Q.* III.iii.40.8	*Poet.* III.i.30 (? parody)
Neaks II.i.54			
Neat III.ii.3	*Gent.* I.iii.10	*Gnat* 119	*Poet.* III.iv.351 (parody)
Nightcrowes I.i.7	*3H6* V.vi.45		
Nuzzled Prol. 16		*F.Q.* I.vi.23.8	
Obloquies IV.iii.91			
Obsequies III.i.20	*Lucr.* 523, *Ham.* V.i.249	*F.Q.* II.i.60.7	
Obtuse I.iii.21			
Opinion IV.i.31	*Ham.* II.i.115	[*F.Q.* II.ii.18.6]	
Outfacing I.iii.58	[*Err.* V.i.244]		
Outmounting* IV.v.56			
Out scout v.iii.62–3			
Paize Prol. 29	[*R3* V.iii.105]	*F.Q.* II.x.5.5	
Palliate II.iii.116	[*LLL.* I.ii.103]		
Pathetically* IV.ii.26	[*R3* IV.i.34]	[*F.Q.* IV.viii.162]	*B.F.* II.v.123
Pent* v.iii.14	*Tim.* IV.i.12	*F.Q.* v.ii.6.8	*Poet.* II.i.26 (parody)
Pils Prol. 5	[*Ant.* III.xii.4]	*S.C.* Oct. 87	
Pinion IV.v.85	*Err.* I.i.73		
Plaining II.iii.129			
Plot v.vi.59	[*MND.* III.i.3]	[*F.Q.* v.ix.47.8]	[*Alc.* I.iii.9]
Plumpe cheekt IV.i.12			
Plunge I.i.44			
Points III.iv.34	*Shr.* III.ii.49		

Polaxes III.i.o.3		*F.Q.* v.xii.14.7	
Poring IV.i.58			
Port holes II.ii.85			
Post II.ii.14			[*Alc.* III.iv.79]
Prate III.iv.17	*Gent.* II.iii.37	*S.C.* Aug. 46	
Presence I.ii.10	*Tp.* II.i.263	*F.Q.* IV.x.14.7	
Proofe II.ii.19	*Meas.* II.iv.29	*F.Q.* I.viii.35.4	
Proud III.ii.2	*R2* I.iii.73	[*F.Q.* IV.x.9.6]	
Puffe I.i.51	*Ant.* II.v.69	*S.C.* Jan. 22	
Pulsiue* IV.iii.46	*Cor.* II.i.230	[*Hymn/Love* 79]	
Purfled I.ii.48		*F.Q.* II.iii.26.5	
Pury* III.iii.51			
Races III.iii.23			
Rackt V.iii.8	*Tw.N* V.i.226	*Hub.* 1306	*Poet.* v.iii.275 (parody)
Ramps* Prol. I			
Range III.ii.8	*Tw.N.* IV.iii.7	*S.C.* Dec. 25	*Sej.* IV.334
Rank* I.v.77			
Rawish* Prol. I			
Refind* IV.v.13			
Respective III.iv.24	*Mer.V.* v.i.156		*Cyn. Rev.* v.iv.229 (parody)
Rheume IV.i.6	*Ham.* II.ii.529		
Rifted II.ii.72	[*Tp.* v.i.45]		
Riueld I.ii.20	*Troil.* v.i.26		
Round Prol. 13			
Routes IV.ii.41	*2H4* IV.iv.9	*F.Q.* I.iv.36.5	
Rozzen III.iv.35			

MARSTON	SHAKESPEARE	SPENSER	JONSON
Saplesse* I.iii.36	[1H6 IV.v.4]	S.C. July 98	
Saw IV.v.82	Ham. I.v.100	F.Q. V.xii.6.8	
Scouts I.i.18	3H6 II.i.116		
Scud IV.iii.103			
Sheathed II.ii.86	Tit. II.i.53	S.C. Sept. 15	
Shotten V.ii9	1H4 II.iv.143	S.C. Aug. 87	
Shrowded IV.iii.17	R3 I.ii.2		
Shrowds II.ii.88	John V.vii.53		
Siddowe* IV.ii.47			
Sighers* IV.iii.197			
Sinking* I.i.76			
Slight brain'd II.v.40			
Slink I.v.96	Tim. IV.ii.11		
Slip I.iii.20	Ven. 515		
Slurd* III.ii.4			
Snarling* Prol. 4			
Snoring* I.i.4	[R3 I.iii.188]		Poet. v.iii.525 (parody)
Solstice I.iii.114	[Tp. II.i.300]		
Sound brain'd IV.i.24			
Spitting IV.i.4	[AYL. V.iii.12]	F.Q. VI.xii.29.5	
Spoke-shaves* IV.v.30			
States I.ii.46	[R2 IV.i.252]		
Staies* IV.iii.8	Oth. IV.ii.170	[Colin 98]	
Sterne bended III.i.45			
Still IV.iii.o.1	Oth. I.iii.95		

Headword			
Stock I.iii.7	Wiv. II.iii.26		
Stone-horse I.iii.33			
Straggling I.ii.21			
Streamers II.i.0.2		F.Q. II.xii.11.5	[B.F. III.ii.118]
Strenuous v.i.3			
Stygian* I.i.89			
Suckets v.v.18			
Surcharg'd II.iii.74			
Surquedries III.ii.72			
Swart III.i.1			
Sweetes I.i.26			
T and I.iii.11	[Tim. v.i.7]		
Tapers I.ii.39	H5 III. Prol. 6		
Tickle II.i.54	[Troil. III.ii.10]	[F.Q. VI.vi.9.8]	Poet. v.iii.292 (parody)
Toplesse I.i.84			Cat. III.389
Traduce II.ii.54	John III.i.46	[F.Q. IV.i.3.4]	
Transshap't* IV.i.3	LLL. IV.iii.114	S.C. Feb. 49	
Troop II.v.37	[Ham. v.i.186]	F.Q. II.x.15.1	
Twines* I.iv.18	Tit. I.i.324	F.Q. I.v.37.6	
Twone II.i.7	2H4 II.i.66	F.Q. I.vi.35.4	
Vnbrac't I.i.0.1	Troil. I.iii.152		
Vnconscionable IV.v.29	Ham. I.iv.18		
Vnequald* I.i.18	[Ado v.i.172]	[F.Q. IV.x.40.8]	
Vnglewd* IV.ii.45		F.Q. III.vi.18.4	
Vnnookt* IV.iii.24	Ham. II.i.78		
Vnpaized* III.i.46			

MARSTON	SHAKESPEARE	SPENSER	JONSON
Vnpeer'd* I.i.10			
Vnpranked* III.ii.5	R3 IV.ii.29		
Vnrespective IV.iii.161			Poet. v.iii.19
Vnsalted IV.ii.43			
Vnseasoned* I.i.37	All's W. I.i.80		
Vnused Prol. 29	Ham. IV.iv.39	F.Q. I.viii.30.7	Poet. III.iii.22 (? parody)
Vnvulgarlie III.iv.43			
Verge* v.vi.35	[R2 II.i.102]		
Vicde* II.ii.41	[Wint. I.ii.416]		
Voids IV.i.5	Mer. V. I.iii.118		
Vouchsafe I.ii.1	Tp. I.ii.422	Colin 939	
Wanton sick II.iii.2			
Well pais'd I.v.97			
Well seasond v.vi.25			
Winde I.iii.90			
Winks Prol. 17	Gent. I.ii.139	F.Q. IV.v.41.3	
Wizard IV.i.45	R3 I.i.56	F.Q. I.iv.12.8	
Word I.iii.34	Ado III.ii.74	F.Q. II.iv.38.4	
Wreake II.iii.94	Rom. III.v.102	Gnat 579	
Wreath* I.ii.16			
Wreath I.v.46	Gent. II.i.19		
Wring I.v.78	Cym. III.vi.79		
Writing tables I.iii.21.1		[F.Q. I.xi.39.2]	
Yawns* III.iii.47	[Ham. III.ii.407]		
Zanie* IV.i.48	Tw.N. I.v.96]